BEING REALISTIC ABOUT REASONS

'a powerful and superbly written short book.'

Barry Maguire, *The Times Literary Supplement*

T. M. Scanlon's new book is essential reading for anybody interested in metaethics and practical rationality. A revised version of the Locke lectures delivered at Oxford in 2009, the book presents Scanlon's distinctive metaethical position, Reasons Fundamentalism, with admirable concision, clarity, and elegance of style. This is the work of a major philosopher at the top of his game.'

Laura Schroeter and François Shroeter, *Ethics*

'a much needed challenge to all forms of non-cognitivism.'

Bruce Russell, *Notre Dame Philosophical Reviews*

BEING
REALISTIC
ABOUT REASONS

T. M. SCANLON

OXFORD
UNIVERSITY PRESS

OXFORD
UNIVERSITY PRESS

Great Clarendon Street, Oxford, OX2 6DP,
United Kingdom

Oxford University Press is a department of the University of Oxford.
It furthers the University's objective of excellence in research, scholarship,
and education by publishing worldwide. Oxford is a registered trade mark of
Oxford University Press in the UK and in certain other countries

First published 2014
First published in paperback 2016

Published in the United States of America by Oxford University Press
198 Madison Avenue, New York, NY 10016, United States of America

British Library Cataloguing in Publication Data
Data available

Library of Congress Cataloging in Publication Data
Data available

ISBN 978–0–19–967848–8 (Hbk.)
ISBN 978–0–19–874810–6 (Pbk.)

For Paul Benacerraf

Preface

This book is a revised version of the John Locke Lectures that I presented in Oxford in the spring of 2009. I am very grateful to the Oxford Faculty of Philosophy for the invitation to give these lectures, which stimulated me to develop my ideas on the subject, and for many fruitful and enjoyable conversations with members of the Faculty while I was in Oxford. I benefitted particularly from conversations with Robert Adams, John Broome, Tom Hurka, Joseph Raz, Ralph Wedgwood, and Tim Williamson.

Since 2009, Lectures 2 and 4 have been heavily revised and extended, and Lecture 5 substantially rewritten. While I have been working on these lectures, a number of very substantial new books have appeared defending positions similar to mine (in particular, similar to, although in some cases subtly different from, the position I take on realism and ontology in Lecture 2.) These include David Enoch's *Taking Morality Seriously*, John Skorupski's *The Domain of Reasons*, Ronald Dworkin's *Justice for Hedgehogs*, and Derek Parfit's *On What Matters*. I have been encouraged by this convergence of opinions, and have tried to take these works into account as best I can. My connection with Parfit's work is particularly close. We have discussed our work in joint seminars on normative realism, and he has given me extensive comments on drafts of these lectures, resulting in significant improvement. As always, I am greatly in his debt.

As I have worked to refine and develop the views on ontology presented in Lecture 2, I have been increasingly struck by similarities of my view to earlier writings by others, including Thomas Nagel, Crispin Wright, Hilary Putnam, and W. W. Tait. Although differences remain in each case, I have learned a great deal from their work and have been encouraged by the thought that, if not in complete agreement with them, I am at least heading in the right direction.

These lectures formed the basis of my Pufendorf Lectures at the University of Lund in 2010, and my Kant Lectures at Stanford in 2012.

An early version of Lecture 1 was presented as the Royal Institute of Philosophy Lecture, and versions of other lectures have been presented as talks at a number of universities. I am grateful to members of these audiences for their comments and questions.

I am particularly grateful to my colleagues, Selim Berker, Peter Koellner, Charles Parsons, and Hilary Putnam for many very helpful and encouraging conversations, and for their extensive written comments on various drafts. Many others have generously sent me written comments or made helpful suggestions, including at least Paul Boghossian, Anthony Brueckner, Tyler Burge, Roger Crisp, Matti Eklund, David Enoch, Solomon Feferman, Kit Fine, Richard Kraut, Thomas Nagel, Włodek Rabinowicz, Michael Ridge, Simon Rippon, Michael Smith, and John Skorupski.

My thanks also to Adam Kern for research assistance, and to Lucy Scanlon for helping with the selection of cover art and in many other ways.

Some of the questions dealt with in these lectures have occupied me for a long time. I have been trying to decide what to think about Carnap's views on ontology ever since writing my senior thesis on mathematical platonism under Paul Benacerraf's supervision in 1962. It was that experience that drew me into philosophy, and I never would have taken it up as a profession were it not for Paul's encouragement and guidance. Without Paul neither this book nor anything else I have done in philosophy would have been written.

Contents

Lecture 1

Introduction: Reasons Fundamentalism

1. Contemporary metaethics differs in two important ways from the metaethics of the 1950s and 1960s, and even the later 1970s, when John Mackie wrote *Ethics: Inventing Right and Wrong*. In that earlier period, discussion in metaethics focused almost entirely on morality: on the proper interpretation of claims about moral right and wrong, and other forms of moral evaluation. Today, although morality is still much discussed, a significant part of the debate concerns practical reasoning and normativity more generally: reasons for action, and, even more broadly, reasons for belief and other attitudes, which are increasingly recognized as normative, and as raising questions of the same nature as those about reasons for action.

The metaethics of the mid-twentieth century also focused on the question of *motivation*. With respect to morality in particular, the question was how agents can be motivated by their moral judgments. In *The Possibility of Altruism*, Thomas Nagel was attacking the prevailing Humean orthodoxy, and he considered requirements of ethics and prudence to be rational requirements. But he nonetheless presented the problem he was addressing as a problem about motivation. Thus he wrote, "I conceive of ethics as a branch of psychology. My claims concern its foundation, or ultimate motivational basis."[1] Today, although motivation is still mentioned, questions are also likely to be put in terms of *reasons*. With respect to prudence and morality, the questions are why a person has reason to do what will benefit him or her in the future, and to do what morality demands.

---

1. *The Possibility of Altruism*, p. 3. (Works will be cited in footnotes only by title. Full publication information can be found in the bibliography.)

It may be tendentious for me to say that metaethics as a field has undergone these two changes. Perhaps they are only changes in my own thinking, or the thinking of those I talk with most frequently. But, whatever may be said about the field as a whole, my approach in these lectures will fall on the second side of each of these dichotomies: my focus will be on normativity in general, treating morality as a special case, and I will be concerned centrally with the idea of a reason— mainly with the idea of a reason for action, although I will have a little to say about reasons of other kinds.

My lectures will offer a qualified defense of a realistic cognitivism about reasons: a view that is cognitivist in holding that claims about reasons for action can be correct or incorrect, but realistic also in recognizing that there may be limits to the range of cases in which such claims have determinate truth values.

I will maintain that truths about reasons are fundamental in the sense that truths about reasons are not reducible to or identifiable with nonnormative truths, such as truths about the natural world of physical objects, causes and effects, nor can they be explained in terms of notions of rationality or rational agency that are not themselves claims about reasons. Reasons might be fundamental in the further sense of being the only fundamental elements of the normative domain, other normative notions such as *good* and *ought* being analyzable in terms of reasons. I am inclined to believe that reasons are indeed fundamental in this further sense. But this belief is controversial, and I will not argue for it in what follows. The Reasons Fundamentalism that I will be defending is just the thesis that reasons are fundamental in the first way I have mentioned.

2. The idea that there are truths about reasons for action is strongly supported by common sense. Consider, for example, the following claims.

(1) For a person in control of a fast moving automobile, the fact that the car will injure and perhaps kill a pedestrian if the wheel is not turned is a reason to turn the wheel.

(2) The fact that a person's child has died is a reason for that person to feel sad.

(3) The fact that it would be enjoyable to listen to some very engaging music, moving one's body gently in time with it, is a reason to do this, or to continue doing it.

These things seem, to me at least, obviously true. But the philosophical thesis that these are irreducibly normative truths may seem unsatisfactory, because it leaves unexplained many things that need explaining. Consider the following questions.

Relational Character: Reasons are reasons *for* an agent. How is this relational character to be understood?

Determinate Truth Values: Are statements about reasons true or false, independent of our opinions about them? Does the idea that there are irreducibly normative truths of this kind have unacceptable metaphysical implications?

Supervenience: How are facts about reasons related to facts about what occurs, and what causes what, in the natural world? Normative facts are not entailed by such natural facts, but at least many normative facts depend on non-normative facts: they vary when non-normative facts vary and cannot vary as long as non-normative facts remain the same. This seems puzzling, and in need of explanation.

Knowledge: If there are irreducibly normative facts about reasons, how can we come to know such facts?

Practical Significance: Judgments about reasons play a different role than other beliefs—such as beliefs about the natural world—in practical reasoning and in the explanation of action. How can they play this role if they are beliefs?

Strength: Reasons have varying strengths. The reason to turn the wheel of the car, for example, is a stronger reason than the reason to go on listening to enjoyable music: the fact that turning the wheel to avoid hitting the pedestrian would interfere with one's enjoyment of the music on the radio is not a sufficient reason not to turn it. So there is a question about what this strength amounts to.

Optionality: Some reasons seem to be "optional": they are merely considerations it makes sense to treat as reasons. Whereas other considerations are non-optional: they provide reasons that should be taken into account, whether or not they are conclusive. The pleasure of listening to music, in the example I just gave, is an optional reason—merely something it makes sense to count as a reason if one decides to do so. Whereas, at least in most circumstances, the fact that doing X would substantially reduce one's risk of an early death is a non-optional reason to do X, whether or not it is conclusive in a given case.

3. All of these questions might seem to be answered by an account of reasons that bases them on desires, such as

(1) X has a reason to do A just in case doing A would promote the fulfillment of some desire that X has

or

(2) X has reason to do A if doing A would promote the fulfillment of a desire that X would have if X were fully aware of the relevant non-normative facts and thinking clearly.

A view of this kind explains the relational character of reasons: reasons are *reasons for* a person who has the relevant desire, or would have such a desire if fully informed and thinking clearly. It might also seem to account for the phenomenon of strength: desires have varying strengths, that is to say, varying motivational power, and a desire theory might hold that one reason is stronger than another just in case the desire on which it is based is stronger in this motivational sense. The fact that some reasons are optional might also be explained by saying that they are reasons for doing something *if you desire or want to do so*, and the idea that some reasons are non-optional would thus be the idea that there are some things that promote the fulfillment of desires that everyone has (or everyone who is fully informed about his or her situation and thinking clearly.)

There also might seem to be no difficulty explaining how we can know what reasons we have according to a view of this kind, since we can, at least sometimes, know what we desire and what would fulfill those desires. And we can explain how reasons can motivate, if desires motivate a person to do what would promote their fulfillment, and if a person who has a reason to do something has a desire that that action would promote the fulfillment of.

Finally, a desire theory might claim to explain the phenomenon of supervenience. At one level, this seems obvious: if the reasons for action that people have are a function of natural facts about their desires and what will promote their fulfillment, then as long as these natural facts remain unchanged, people's reasons for action will remain the same as well.

The ability to explain these aspects of reasons is, I believe, a large part of what makes desire-based accounts appealing. There are, however, well-known difficulties with accounts of this kind. Some of these difficulties concern the counterintuitive implications of desire theories about what reasons people have. Does a person really have a reason to do what will fulfill any desire he or she has, not matter how foolish? Does the reason the driver has to turn the car really depend on his or her having a desire that would be fulfilled by doing this? These problems might be lessened by shifting from actual desires to informed desires, and making suitable assumptions about what people would desire if fully informed. But this move brings problems of its own for the desire view's account of motivation, since it is less obvious that people are always motivated by the fact that an action would promote the fulfillment of desires if these are desires that they do not have, but only would have under different conditions.

I believe that substantive objections of this kind count strongly against desire theories of reasons. But I want to set these objections aside for the moment, and instead consider what may seem to be a deeper objection, which claims that the explanatory potential of these theories is in an important respect illusory. The illusion arises from the fact that desire theories can be understood in two very different ways, and statements of these theories often do not clearly distinguish between them.

One way in which it is natural to understand desire theories is as substantive normative claims about what reasons people have. It may be quite plausible to claim (in many cases) that people have reason to do what will promote the satisfaction of their desires. Such a theory could explain some features of reasons for action, such as the relational nature of such reasons, and their strength, in the ways I have mentioned. (Although the idea that the strength of a reason to do something is proportional to its motivational effectiveness does not seem very plausible.) But since a normative desire theory is itself just a very general normative claim, it does not seem to address many of the other questions I have listed.

If there are serious metaphysical problems about the idea of irreducibly normative truths, a normative desire theory would not respond to these worries because it is itself a normative truth of this kind. Nor would a normative desire theory provide a general explanation of how we can come to know normative truths. It simply makes a general substantive claim about reasons for action—that we have reason to do whatever satisfies our desires—which, if true, leaves us only with the empirical problem of figuring out which actions will do this. In the same way, the thesis that the only thing we have reason to do is to get as much money as possible would leave us just with the problem of figuring out how to get rich. It would not solve the problem of how we can come to know normative truths, but would simply offer one such truth, which it claims we know. These points might be summed up by saying that normative desire theories are not rivals to Reasons Fundamentalism but are quite compatible with it. Perhaps they even presuppose it.

An alternative interpretation of a desire theory would take that theory to offer not a normative claim about reasons for action but rather a reductive claim, according to which for *p* to be a reason for an agent to do *a* just is for the truth of *p* to help explain how doing *a* would promote the satisfaction of some desire that the agent has.[2]

Interpreted in this way, a desire theory might provide answers to some of the questions I have listed. It would respond to metaphysical worries about irreducibly normative truths by holding that facts about reasons for action are just a kind of natural fact. And it would respond to epistemological worries as well, by holding that we can come to know truths about reasons for action through the usual kinds of empirical inquiry.

The question, however, would be whether identifying facts about reasons with non-normative facts would explain reasons or eliminate their normativity. The "action guiding" force of reasons, on such a theory, would seem to be purely causal and explanatory. If the fact that one has a strong reason not to do *a* (and no countervailing reason to do *a*) is just a natural fact about what will satisfy one's desires, then this fact might explain one's failure to do *a*. But it does not explain why believing that one has such a reason (believing that this natural fact obtains) can make it irrational for one to do *a*.

A reductive desire theorist might reply, as Mark Schroeder does, that all normativity is to be understood in terms of the idea of a reason. So if it is true that *a person's having a reason just consists in some fact about that person's desires and what will promote them*, a reductive desire theory preserves normativity, since it preserves the idea of a reason.[3] So the question is whether this reductive claim should be accepted. I myself believe that this claim is refuted by the evident lack of intrinsic normative significance of facts about desires. But simply asserting that this is so may seem to lead to a standoff. To move beyond this standoff, one needs to consider and assess the evidence offered in support of the reductive thesis. In Schroeder's case, much depends on his claim that facts about desires, rather than, say, about what a person would enjoy, are the best explanation of the reasons that one person (who likes dancing) has to go to a party

---

2. As Mark Schroeder argues in *Slaves of the Passions*.
3. See *Slaves of the Passions*, pp. 79–83.

where there will be dancing (as compared to the reasons of another person, who does not like to dance).[4] This claim does not strike me as plausible. Pursuing the matter here would take me too far afield, but I will take up the question in my next lecture.

It seems, then, that desire theories face a dilemma: either they begin with a normative claim about reasons for action, in which case they do not explain the features of reasons that may seem puzzling; or else they make a reductive claim, which eliminates normativity altogether. This raises two questions. The first is whether there is any way of understanding the appeal of a desire theory that avoids this dilemma. The second is whether explanations of the kind offered by normative desire theories are as unsatisfactory as they seem. I believe that a normative desire theory is unsatisfactory, but not for the reasons I have just been discussing—not because of its lack of explanatory depth. I will return to this question in Lecture 4.

4. A different way of explaining truths about reasons holds that reasons can be grounded in an idea of rationality. A rationality-based account has the following general form:

(3) The fact that p is a reason for a person to do a when and because rationality requires such a person to count this fact in favor of doing a.

The right hand side of this formula employs the idea of a reason—the idea of counting a consideration *in favor of* an action. But what it employs is just the idea of an agent's *treating* something as a reason. It thus involves no appeal to conclusions (arrived at independently) about what reasons people actually have. The work in this formula is done instead by the concept of rationality, which is taken to support such conclusions.

There is a familiar sense of "rational" in which the rational thing to do is just the thing that is required or supported by the reasons one has or, perhaps, by the reasons one would have, if one's other beliefs were true. People use "rational" in this sense when, for example, they claim that it is rational to do what is in one's self-interest (or would be in one's self-interest if one's other beliefs were true). Such a thesis does not explain claims about reasons in terms of rationality, but rather presupposes, or asserts, claims about what reasons people have.

4. *Slaves of the Passions*, Chapters 1 and 8.

A rationality-based account of reasons would be trivial, and fail in its aim of explaining the idea of a reason for action, if it appealed to a notion of rationality of this sort. So an account of reasons of the kind I am considering must employ a conception of rationality that does not consist of or depend on a substantive conception of the reasons people have.

In a Kantian theory, which is the most familiar view of this type, the fundamental claim is that the Categorical Imperative is a condition of rationality. The claim is that anyone who sees him or herself as a rational agent must, on pain of irrationality, see the Categorical Imperative as the fundamental principle of practical reasoning. A consideration *p* is a reason for an agent to do *a*, according to this theory, if a failure to count this fact as a reason to do *a* would be incompatible with the Categorical Imperative. So far, this seems to cover only moral reasons, broadly construed. Christine Korsgaard's version of a Kantian view extends this by adding that the fact that *p* is a reason for an agent to do *a* if failing to see it as such a reason is incompatible with some "practical identity" that the agent has adopted (and adopting that identity is itself compatible with the Categorical Imperative).[5]

Consider now how a view that bases claims about reasons on requirements of rationality might explain some of the puzzling features of reasons that I mentioned above. A view of this kind can explain what I called above the relational character of facts about reasons, since such facts are, on this view, facts about what an agent can (consistent with rationality) treat as a reason. It can also explain what makes claims about reasons correct when they are correct: they are correct if they do indeed follow from requirements of rationality. We can know what reasons we have, on such an account, because we can know what rationality requires, and insofar as we are rational we will be moved to do what have reason to do. The "strength" of reasons can be explained in what might be called a "top down" fashion, in contrast to the "bottom up" explanation offered by a desire theory. It is not that reasons "come with" particular strengths, as they would on a desire-based view. Rather, one consideration is a stronger reason than another if it would be irrational to refrain from doing what the former reason counts in favor of because the latter reason counts against so acting.

It is less clear how a rationality-based view should explain the optional character of some reasons. But I will leave this aside for now

---

5. See *The Sources of Normativity,* esp. pp. 102–7, 239–42. For a non-Kantian view that bases reasons on rationality see Joshua Gert, *Brute Rationality: Normativity and Human Action.*

in order to consider what has been seen as one of the main advantages of such a view over rival accounts, such as Reasons Fundamentalism.

This concerns what Christine Korsgaard calls "The Normative Question," of how reasons acquire their normative force or, as she sometimes puts it, how reasons "get a grip on" an agent. A view of the kind I am calling Reasons Fundamentalism, which takes there to be facts about which things are reasons, cannot, she says, give a satisfactory answer to this question. If a consideration's being a reason for a person is just another fact about the world, she says, then the person could still be perfectly indifferent to this fact.[6]

What kind of grip is in question here? If it were the "grip" or authority that moral conclusions are thought to have over us, then this could be intelligibly explained by offering reasons to do what morality requires. But the move from morality to reasons in general rules out such an answer. The authority of conclusions about reasons for action cannot be explained by giving a further reason since the same question would arise over again about this reason.

We might say that the Normative Question is a question of motivation. But here we need to distinguish several different issues. On the one hand, there is the question of how a person can be motivated by the thought that some fact is a reason for action if this thought is a mere belief that something is the case. This is the problem coming down to us from Hume. I believe that, as I will argue in Lecture 3, the idea of rational agency provides an answer to this question, which might be called the internal question of motivation. I will not discuss this question here, however, since I do not believe it is the question that Korsgaard has in mind.

A second way of understanding Korsgaard's Normative Question in terms of motivation would be to see it as what might be called an external question of motivation—a question about how the fact that p is a reason for an agent to do a, if it is just a fact, could get the agent to accept that p is a reason to do a and treat it as such. The agent could simply deny that it is a reason. If he did, what could we say to him? A Reasons Fundamentalist, Korsgaard might say, would simply insist that p is after all a reason, and that is all there is to it.[7] This is obviously not going to move the person who denies it.

---

6. *The Sources of Normativity*, pp. 44–6.   7. *The Sources of Normativity*, p. 38.

The challenge here is not, I think, correctly described as a question of motivation if that is understood to mean a question that might be answered by a psychological explanation of how a person could be moved to respond to a fact in a certain way. The problem is not a matter of motivation in this psychological sense, but rather of something more like normative authority. The question is not how an agent might come to respond to the fact that *p* is a reason for her to do *a*, by accepting that it is a reason, but rather a question of why, if she does have these reasons, she *must* so respond. That is why she calls it "the *normative* question."

Korsgaard is quite correct about what a Reasons Fundamentalist, or at least *this* Reasons Fundamentalist, would say in a situation of the kind she imagines. According to a Reasons Fundamentalist, the relation that holds between an agent and a consideration *p* in such a situation just *is* the relation of *p*'s *being a reason for that agent to do a*. The "grip" that this has on the agent just is this relation: *being a reason for* him or her (or, in the strongest cases, a conclusive reason).[8] As Korsgaard puts it, quite correctly, a Reasons Fundamentalist "insists on the irreducible character of normativity."[9] The fundamental disagreement here concerns whether some further explanation can and should be given of why the agent in this situation *must* treat *p* as a reason.

Korsgaard believes that in order to explain the force of this "must," we have to find something *about the agent* in virtue of which she must accept that *p* is a reason for her to do *a*. Whatever plays this role can't just be another truth about what reasons the person has, or else the whole problem would begin again. But in order to have normative force, the explanation we are looking for can't just be a psychological principle. It follows that the problem can be solved only by finding a kind of normativity—some grounding for a "must"—that does not start from a claim about which things are reasons. Korsgaard finds this in the idea of rational agency itself. As she puts it, "Kantians believe that the source of the normativity of moral claims must be found in the agent's own will."[10] I believe that what she here says explicitly about moral claims is in her view true of all claims about reasons. Claims about moral requirements are grounded in things that an agent must accept insofar as she sees

---

8. For a similar statement see R. Jay Wallace, "Normativity and the Will," pp. 75–6.
9. *The Sources of Normativity*, p. 32.   10. *The Sources of Normativity*, p. 19.

herself as acting at all. Other reasons are things that an agent "must" see as reasons in virtue of some more specific identity that she has.

5. The idea that claims about the reasons an agent has must be grounded in something that is already true of that agent (or of that agent's own attitudes) is shared by a surprisingly wide range of views, many of them not at all Kantian. I am tempted to say, although it would no doubt be an exaggeration, that it is shared by almost all those who believe in normative reasons but are not Reasons Fundamentalists.

Consider, for example, Gilbert Harman's view.[11] Harman writes that an agent's reasons for action must follow from his or her "goals, desires or intentions." He does not put it this way, but it seems in the spirit of his view to add that claims about reasons that are not so based fail to "get a grip on the agent." I believe that something similar might be said by proponents of desire-based views more generally, such as Bernard Williams' view that the only valid claims about reasons are what he calls internal reason statements—that is, claims about what could be reached by a sound deliberative route from the agent's actual subjective motivational set.[12]

Williams' idea of a "sound deliberative route" allows that a consideration can be a reason for an agent even though the agent is not presently motivated by that consideration. It is enough that being so motivated has the right kind of connection with the agent's present attitudes. This connection might be described in terms of motivation, but it seems to me at base a *normative* connection, as indicated in the fact that what is in question is a *sound* deliberative route.[13] What the soundness of this route does is to ground the reason normatively in something to which the agent is already committed, thereby making it something the agent cannot deny without irrationality.

Another claim that Williams once made may be relevant here. Arguing against proponents of "external" reasons, he said that there are many criticisms that might be brought against a man who treats his wife badly and does not care at all about this—he may be cruel,

---

11. As expressed in "Moral Relativism Defended."
12. See his "Internal and External Reasons."
13. I said earlier in discussing desire-based views that the move from an actual desire account to one based on informed desires might involve sacrificing the connection with motivation that is one of the hallmarks of desire theories. The fact that desire theorists are not troubled by this move may support the point I am making—that what may be described as motivation is actually a matter of rational connection.

heartless, and so on, and it might be better if he were not like this. But a defender of "external reasons" statements, Williams said, wants to go beyond this and say that the man is *irrational* if he fails to recognize that he has a reason to treat his wife differently.[14] A defender of external reasons need not make this claim, as Williams later recognized.[15] But I conjecture that Williams made the claim in the first place because he himself believed that claims about reasons must "get a grip on the agent" in a way that would ground a charge of irrationality if the agent ignored these reasons. He therefore thought that his opponent would want to claim this as well.

A similar thought seems to be what draws Michael Smith, in *The Moral Problem*, to identify reasons with what a person would desire for him or herself if fully rational.[16] The fact that the reason is determined by what *that person* would desire if fully rational (fully informed, thinking clearly, and so on) ensures a connection with the agent him or herself, perhaps close enough to make it irrational for the person to reject the reason. As Smith has said more recently, "If morality requires some limited form of altruism then…the principle of limited altruism is a principle…on all fours with *modus ponens* and *modus tollens* and the principle of means-ends."[17] Here again, the idea seems to be that claims about the reasons an agent has, if correct, must be claims that the agent cannot deny without irrationality.

The idea of grounding claims about an agent's reasons in attitudes that that agent already holds may derive some of its appeal from the dialectical context in which argument about reasons for action is imagined to take place. In Williams' example of the man who sees no reason to treat his wife better, the context is an instance of what Gilbert Harman calls "external reasoning," a context in which two people are arguing about what reasons for action one of them has.[18] In such a context, facts about one party's actual attitudes (as opposed to the merits of the content of those attitudes) have a particular salience. It is an obvious dialectical advantage to be able to "get a grip" on your

14. "Internal and External Reasons," p. 110. Korsgaard makes a similar suggestion about what a realist might claim in "Acting for a Reason," p. 213.
15. In "Replies," p. 192.
16. *The Moral Problem*, pp. 151ff.
17. "Objectivity and Moral Realism: On the Significance of the Phenomenology of Moral Experience," p. 250.
18. Harman, "Notes on Practical Reasoning," p. 3.

opponent by saying: "But you accept that…and it follows from this that the fact that *p* counts in favor of *phi*-ing."

It is noteworthy, I think, that much of Williams' discussion in "Internal and External Reasons" involves cases in which one person is trying to force some other person to agree that he has a reason to act in a certain way. (The example just mentioned, of the man who treats his wife badly, is a case in point; the Owen Wingrave example is another.[19] These are, I think, typical.) Part of Korsgaard's argument early in *The Sources of Normativity* assumes a similar dialectical situation. She imagines two people disagreeing about whether something is a reason for a certain action, and she observes that it is mere reiterative stone-kicking for one party to say, in the face of the other's denial, "But it just *is* a reason!"[20] A much more effective response would be to come up with an argument that begins from something that the other party accepts, or cannot deny on pain of irrationality.

But what it takes for a claim to be correct need not be the same as what it takes for the claim to be one that one's opponent in argument cannot consistently deny. These two things are certainly different with respect to claims about empirical facts, and I believe they are also different with respect to claims about reasons, which is the matter at issue. That they are different is strongly suggested when we shift to what Harman calls a case of "internal reasoning," which is reasoning about what reasons one has oneself. In this case, the mere fact that one cannot consistently reject a claim about reasons given that one has some desire, intention, or other attitude does not itself settle the matter. One can always ask oneself why one should have these attitudes—whether they can be justified in the relevant way. From the agent's own point of view his or her own attitudes are largely transparent to the subject matter under consideration.

Korsgaard recognizes, indeed emphasizes, the possibility of this kind of reflective "stepping back" when one is thinking about what reasons one has. In such a situation, she says, a person must keep on asking "why" until she comes to a point at which it is "impossible, unnecessary or incoherent to ask why again."[21] This is what she calls the search for the unconditioned. But, leaving aside whether it is possible to find an unconditioned starting point for reasoning about what reasons one has (a starting point that does not itself involve some substantive judgment about reasons), must we always seek such a starting point? The claim that we must continue stepping back until it is "impossible, unnecessary or incoherent to ask why again" would be much less plausible without the disjunct "unnecessary." But when is it unnecessary to ask any further? I would say that this depends on the substantive merits of the answer one has reached—on whether this answer is clearly correct, or whether there is any reason to doubt it.

Grounding claims about reasons in claims about rationality (that is to say, claims about what is required to avoid *irrationality*) thus has greatest appeal in the case of external reasoning. In internal reasoning what comes to the fore are substantive conclusions about the subject matter being dealt with—in this case reasons about what to do. There is a reversal here that may at first seem surprising, but should not be so. Claims about irrationality are in one sense more internal than substantive claims about reasons. As John Broome says, they depend only on the contents of the subject's own mind.[22] But such claims are not as relevant in internal reasoning as in the external variety, and it is the point of view of internal reasoning that is primary in an investigation of reasons and normativity. From this point of view the question of how reasons "get a grip on one" properly disappears. There is only the question: what reasons do I have?

6. In these introductory remarks I have tried, first, to identify the position for which I will offer a qualified defense: claims about reasons can be correct or incorrect, and such claims are fundamental—not reducible to or explainable in terms of claims of other kinds. I have tried to identify this position in a way that brings out what seems unsatisfactorily incomplete about such an account. I have considered two ways of providing a fuller explanation of reasons, by basing them in desires or in an idea of rationality. I have explained briefly why I find these unsatisfactory, and I will have more to say about this in later lectures. If these explanations are unsatisfactory, and if, as I will argue in the next two lectures, the appeal of expressivist views should be resisted, then unless there is some other general account of reasons (which I doubt) Reasons Fundamentalism will be left as the only available position.

---

22. Broome, "Does Rationality Consist in Responding Correctly to Reasons?"

Even if this is so, however, the various problems about reasons that I have listed still remain to be answered. In my next lecture, I will argue, in the light of a general view of ontological questions, that the idea of irreducibly normative truths presents no metaphysical problem. I will also present an account of the relation between normative and non-normative facts which, I believe, explains the phenomena of covariance and supervenience. In Lecture 3, I will argue that an account of judgments about reasons for action that interprets them as a kind of belief can still explain the practical significance of such judgments and their role in the explanation of action. In Lecture 4, I will take up the related questions of how normative statements can be true independent of us and how we can have knowledge of such truths. Finally, in Lecture 5, I will offer an interpretation of the strength of practical reasons, and explain in what sense reasons can be "optional."

Lecture 2
Metaphysical Objections

1. As I said in my first lecture, the idea that there are irreducibly normative truths about reasons for action, which we can discover by thinking carefully about reasons in the usual way, has been thought to be subject to three kinds of objections: metaphysical, epistemological, and motivational or, as I would prefer to say, practical. Metaphysical objections claim that a belief in irreducibly normative truths would commit us to facts or entities that would be metaphysically odd—incompatible, it is sometimes said, with a scientific view of the world. Epistemological objections maintain that if there were such truths we would have no way of discovering them. Practical objections maintain that if conclusions about what we have reason to do were simply beliefs in a kind of fact, they could not have the practical significance that reasons are commonly supposed to have. This is often put by saying that beliefs alone cannot motivate an agent to act. I think the objection is better put as the claim that beliefs cannot explain action, or make acting rational or irrational in the way that accepting conclusions about reasons is normally thought to do. I will concentrate in this lecture on metaphysical objections.

Stating his version of this objection, John Mackie writes that, "if there were objective values, then they would be entities or qualities or relations of a very strange sort, utterly different from anything else in the universe."[1] Others have made similar objections. It is natural to

---

1. *Ethics: Inventing Right and Wrong*, p. 38. In fairness to Mackie, I should note that, like most people discussing these issues at the time he was writing, he was concerned with morality, not with practical reasons more generally. When he speaks of claims about objective values, he may intend to contrast these with claims about "subjective" values—claims about what a person ought to do, or has reason to do, that, unlike moral claims, are claimed to hold only insofar as the agent has certain desires or aims. Mackie may have no objection to values, or claims about reasons, of the latter kind.

If so, however, his position suffers a certain instability. As I have pointed out in my first lecture, the claim that a person has reason to do what will promote the satisfaction

describe this as an ontological objection: that the idea that there are irreducibly normative truths has implications that are incompatible with plausible views about "what there is." I do not believe that the supposed problem here is one of ontology. But it will be helpful to consider the matter first in this ontological form.

In his famous essay "On What There Is" Quine proposed that we understand what he called our "ontological commitments" in the following way. The ontological commitments of a set of statements are determined by first translating these statements into the language of first-order logic, and then determining what existential claims follow from these statements. These existential claims express what we are ontologically committed to in accepting those statements.

Quine's criterion itself says nothing about what ontology we have reason to accept. It says nothing about whether and how we should be concerned with our ontological commitments: whether we should, for example, avoid ontological commitment to anything other than physical objects, or should limit our ontology as much as possible. An ontological objection to normative truths depends on some restrictive view of this kind. Mackie's objection seems to be based on the view that all of our ontological commitments must be understood as claims about what exists in the physical world of space and time. This world is the "universe" that he has in mind when he says that objective values would involve entities, qualities, or relations "different from anything else *in the universe.*" The same assumption lies behind the frequently-heard charge that the idea that there are irreducibly normative truths is incompatible with a scientific view of the world. This idea, that our ontological commitments should be restricted to things in the physical world of particles and planets that is described by science, may strike many as a sensible naturalism. But it is an idea we should not accept.

---

of his or her desires is itself a normative claim. Indeed, it is an "objective" normative claim, since it does not *itself* depend on what people desire, or on what aims they have. If there is something *metaphysically* odd about objective normative truths, then this supposed truth (that people have reason to do what would satisfy their desires, or promote their aims) is just as odd as any other. The disagreement between someone who thinks that all reasons for action depend on the agent's desires and someone who thinks that there are some reasons that do not depend on agents' desires is a *normative* disagreement, not a metaphysical one. So Mackie's "argument from queerness," insofar as the queerness involved is metaphysical, is an argument against irreducibly normative truths of any kind, not just objective moral values. At least this is how I am going to take his argument, I hope not unfairly.

Science is a way of understanding the natural world. Its conclusions represent our best understanding of what that world contains and what happens in it. Accepting science as the way of understanding the natural world entails rejecting claims about this world that are incompatible with science, such as claims about witches and spirits. But accepting a scientific view of the natural world does not mean accepting the view that the only meaningful statements with determinate truth values are statements about the natural world, or that things in the natural world are the only things we should be ontologically committed to in Quine's sense.

In Quine's case, exclusive emphasis on the physical world is built in from the start. His concern is exclusively with theories of the world that impinges on our sensory surfaces. This immediately excludes the normative, absent some naturalistic reduction. It might seem also to exclude ontological commitments to mathematical entities such as numbers and sets (again, absent some naturalistic reduction). But Quine's holism treats mathematical and logical truths as the most abstract parts of our theory of the world, which faces the tribunal of sensory experience as a whole. Whether the best such theory should quantify over numbers or sets is a scientific question about what the best (most successful and simplest) overall scientific theory is like. Thus, speaking of the suggestion by some logicians that "all the mathematical needs of science can be supplied on the meager basis of what has come to be known as predicative set theory," Quine writes that "Such gains are of a piece with the simplifications and economies that are hailed as progress within natural science itself. It is a matter of tightening and streamlining our global system of the world."[2]

There is something odd about this view. It sounds odd to say that the physical world *contains* numbers and sets, in addition to particles and mountains and planets. Quine does not say this. But if numbers and sets are not part of the natural world, and if there are serious onto-logical objections to the idea that such things exist, then it is difficult to see how the usefulness of quantifying numbers and sets could justify genuine commitment to their existence, as opposed to a kind of fictionalism: a practice of merely speaking *as* if there were such things. I will return to this question.

---

2. *The Pursuit of Truth*, p. 95.

I believe that the way of thinking about these matters that makes most sense is a view that does not privilege science but takes as basic a range of domains, including mathematics, science, and moral and practical reasoning. It holds that statements within all of these domains are capable of truth and falsity, and that the truth values of statements about one domain, insofar as they do not conflict with statements of some other domain, are properly settled by the standards of the domain that they are about. Mathematical questions, including questions about the existence of numbers and sets are settled by mathematical reasoning, scientific questions, including questions about the existence of bosons, by scientific reasoning, normative questions by normative reasoning, and so on.[3] This view requires clarification in several respects.

The first clarification concerns the idea of a domain.[4] If we take arithmetic or set theory as primary examples of domains, then it is tempting to think of a domain as consisting of a realm of objects of a certain kind and their properties. But this would be misleading. The normative domain, for example, is not a distinct realm of objects. Things in the natural world, such as persons and their actions, have normative properties, and most normative claims are claims about such things. Even in the case of arithmetic, although there are pure claims about numbers, there are also numerical claims about the physical world. So a domain is better understood in terms of the kind of claims it involves, and hence in terms of concepts that it deals with, such as number, set, physical object, reason, or morally right action.

---

3. My view has obvious similarities with Carnap's, as expressed in "Empiricism, Semantics, and Ontology." In contrast to Carnap, however, I do not take the procedures appropriate to a domain to be determined by "linguistic rules" for the use of the terms in question. People can use terms such as "number," "set," or "wrongness" without misuse of language while disagreeing to some degree about the facts about such things, and about the best ways of determining these facts. Nor do I hold, as Carnap did, that the standards of a domain always have the last word on questions about the existence of objects that are quantified over in that domain, and that there are no meaningful theoretical questions about whether such objects exist. As I go on to say in the text, I believe that there can be meaningful external questions about a domain. But these must be questions about whether the implications or presuppositions of statements internal to the domain are fulfilled.

4. A number of others have used the term, "domain" in very much the way I am using it here. See, in particular, W. W. Tait, in "Truth and Proof: The Platonism of Mathematics," "Beyond the Axioms: The Question of Objectivity in Mathematics," and his introduction to *The Provenance of Pure Reason: Essays in the Philosophy of Mathematics and Its History*; Ronald Dworkin, in *Justice for Hedgehogs*; and John Skorupski, in *The Domain of Reasons*.

A second clarification concerns the idea of the standards for answering questions within a domain. There are mathematical standards for answering mathematical questions, scientific standards for answering empirical questions about the physical world, and forms of practical reasoning for answering questions about what we have reason to do. These standards typically consist, in part, of substantive principles about the domain, such as mathematical axioms, moral principles, and scientific generalizations. But these substantive standards are justified by less explicitly codified reasoning about the subject matter in question, and they can be revised in the light of further reasoning of this kind. For example, reasoning about the concept of a set can lead to changes in the accepted axioms of set theory, and reasoning about the ideas of moral right and wrong can lead to changes in accepted moral theories and moral principles.

As these examples indicate, this reasoning is itself internal to the domains in question. It proceeds by appeal to our best general understanding of the nature of the concepts basic to the domain in question and to the most obvious particular truths within it. (I will say more about this kind of reasoning in Lecture 4.) The standards comprising what we call "scientific method" are justified by, on the one hand, our conception of the subject matter of science—that it is comprised of objects in space, causally interacting with us ("impinging on our sensory surfaces" as Quine says). It is also supported by the demonstrated success of the methods of empirical science in predicting and explaining what seem to us obvious facts about this world. The details of this process—in particular, the role of causal interaction and hence of sensory observation—are peculiar to this domain. But the general structure of the process is the same in other domains. When I say that the truth values of statements within a domain are properly settled by the standards and reasoning internal to that domain I mean to be including reasoning of all of these kinds, not just the particular substantive principles about the subject matter of a domain that we accept at a given time.

The two final clarifications concern conflicts between statements of one domain and those of another. The thesis that the truth values of statements in a domain, including existential statements, are properly settled by standards internal to that domain applies only to what I will call pure statements in a domain, not to mixed statements, which also make claims about other domains. In the case of number theory and set theory, pure statements are statements that employ (as non-logical elements) only concepts peculiar to that domain. In the case of normative statements the matter is more complicated, since normative statements make claims about the normative significance of natural facts and properties. So, for example, the claim that a certain action is morally wrong might involve not only the claim that any action having certain consequences would be wrong but also that this action actually has those consequences. The truth of such a claim would therefore depend on empirical, as well as moral reasoning. I will have more to say about pure vs. mixed claims later in this lecture.

My final clarification is that this domain-centered view does not hold that first-order domains are entirely autonomous, and that nothing beyond the (evolving) standards of a domain can be relevant to the truth of statements within it. Even pure statements in one domain can entail or presuppose claims in some other domain, and when this happens these claims need to be reconciled, and some of them modified or given up. We might, for example, have a first-order theory of witches and spirits. That is, we might have established criteria for deciding whether someone is or is not a witch, and whether or not a ghost is present. But such conclusions entail claims about events in the physical world and their causes: about what causes, or can cause, cows to stop giving milk, and people to become sick and die. These claims conflict with claims of physics and other empirical sciences, and this conflict provides decisive reason to reject the idea that there are witches and spirits.[5]

To put the same point more generally: there can be meaningful "external" questions about the adequacy of the reasoning in a domain, and about the truth of statements, including existential statements, that these modes of reasoning support. Meaningful questions of this kind are questions about whether the modes of reasoning in a domain actually support all the conclusions that are required in order for statements employing the concepts of that domain to be true and to have the significance that is claimed for them. These questions are "external" to the domain insofar as they cannot be settled by the modes of

---

5. My view is thus not open to the objection that Hartry Field raises, unfairly I believe, against Crispin Wright's similar view when Field charges that giving priority to "ordinary criteria" would require us to accept such things as that God exists and that Zeus throws thunderbolts. See Field, "Platonism for Cheap? Crispin Wright on Frege's Context Principle," p. 155.

reasoning of that domain. But these questions are made relevant by their relation to claims that are internal to the domain itself.

Sometimes, as in the case of witches and spirits, these external questions are questions about the natural world, to be settled by scientific criteria. Some claims about gods may involve claims of this kind, such as claims about the creation of the universe, or about what is happening when lightning occurs. An interpretation of moral claims, or claims about reasons for action that takes these claims to be straightforwardly true would be "incompatible with a scientific view of the world" if these normative claims entailed, or if their supposed significance presupposed, claims about the natural world that science gives us good reasons to reject. But pure normative statements do not involve or presuppose such claims. Nor, as I will argue in Lecture 4, does the possibility of our coming to know normative truths involve claims about causal interaction with normative facts, properties, or entities. Nor does the possibility of agents being motivated by their beliefs about normative facts involve causal interaction with these facts. It is true, however, that normative claims would not have the significance that we normally attribute to them if there were no rational agents. So the existence of such agents is a presupposition of the practical domain that could in principle be undermined by external argument. I do not believe that it is in fact undermined in this way, since I believe that rational agents are just a kind of natural organism, and that organisms of this kind do exist.

Morality has external presuppositions of a different kind. The claims that we make about moral right and wrong generally presuppose that there are moral standards that everyone has good reason to take seriously as guides to conduct and as standards for objecting to what others do. But the ordinary ways of understanding morality, and ordinary ways of arguing for moral conclusions do not make clear what these reasons are, or establish that we have such reasons. There is therefore a question, external to morality, whether the usual ways of establishing that a form of conduct is wrong also guarantee that there are good reasons not to engage in it. This question is not scientific or metaphysical but normative—a question about what we have reason to do.

On the view I am proposing, we should decide what existential statements to accept simply by applying the criteria relevant to various domains, taking into account the interaction between different domains of the kind I have just been describing. I have been mentioning, as examples, the domains of mathematics and of normative truths because these are frequently discussed as raising ontological issues. But I mean to leave the question of what domains there are entirely open.[6] The idea of domains, like Carnap's related idea of frameworks, may seem to be a piece of philosophical apparatus that is in need of justification, and may even raise ontological issues. But the question about domains is not whether they exist but whether they provide a helpful way of discussing certain matters. The term "domain" as I am using it is just a way of referring to the fact that statements can make claims about different subjects: some make claims about the natural world, some make claims about numbers, some make claims about reasons. This is a common-sense idea. Even the idea that questions about a given domain (i.e. about a given subject) should be settled by the best ways of thinking about that subject is a piece of common sense, even a triviality. This becomes philosophically controversial only when it is combined with the claim that statements about domains other than the natural world should be seen as autonomous in the way I have described.

Even though there can be meaningful external questions about claims within a domain, we have no reasons to be concerned with our general ontological commitments in Quine's sense, that is to say with the totality of things the existence of which is entailed by all the statements (in any domain) that we accept as true.

I am not denying that we can form a coherent idea of a domain concerned with the general idea of existence that applies to everything we are committed to quantifying over in a range of particular domains. Unless more is said about it, however, this perfectly general idea of existence seems empty, in contrast to the significance, and "thickness," that ideas of existence within the particular domains I have mentioned can have.

As Tait says, this merely disjunctive "universe" in which something exists if it is a physical object, or a number or is entailed by true statements of some other domain, is entirely parasitic on the particular

---

6. There is also the question of whether the particular domains I have listed are in fact single, unified domains. For example, do all the entities referred to in various parts of mathematics belong to a single, unified "world" of abstract objects or are distinct domains corresponding to various subfields of mathematics. This is a substantive question, on which I do not here need to take a position, about how the subject matters of those subfields are best understood. I am grateful to Charles Parsons for calling this question to my attention.

domains that contribute to it.[7] That is, it provides no bases for standards of existence beyond those of these particular domains: no domain-
independent reason to want to minimize these commitments, for
example, and no reason in general to limit these commitments to con-
crete entities as opposed to abstract ones.

To put this point in a slightly different way, our ontological commitments in this general sense do not represent a claim on our part about
what *the world* contains, in any meaningful sense of "the world." To say
that it does invites, first, worries like Mackie's, which arise from taking
these to be commitments about the natural world, i.e. the physical
universe.[8] And if we respond to this first worry by denying that numbers, say, are part of the natural world, while still insisting that they are
part of "the world" we invite questions about what this shadowy
"world" is to which numbers and perhaps other non-spatial entities all
belong.[9] It is better to avoid such questions altogether.[10]

7. Tait writes, "Naturally, one can always stipulate that what one means by 'existence' is
   the disjunction of existences over a range of domains of discourse. But, beyond the
   question of separating out those domains which one should take seriously from the
   rest, this notion of existence is parasitic off the various domain-relative notions of
   existence" (*The Provenance of Pure Reason*, p. 8).
8. As John McDowell observed, Mackie's argument "involves a tendentious use of 'the
   world.'" "Values and Secondary Qualities," p. 185, note 36. See also the beginning of
   McDowell's "Non-Cognitivism and Rule Following."
9. People holding positions similar to the one I favor also sometimes state their claims in
   terms that may invite Mackie's response. Wright, for example writes that if natural
   number is a sortal concept then "its instances, if it has any, will thus be *objects*, furnishings of the world every bit as objective as mountains, rivers and trees" (*Frege's Conception of Numbers as Objects*, p. 13). My view about the criteria of existence for numbers
   and other non-spatio-temporal objects is very close to Wright's. But saying that these
   things are "furnishings of the world" seems to me misleading, and unnecessarily to
   invite a response like Mackie's. On the other hand, while I am in broad agreement
   with John Skorupski's view, particularly with his view that normative propositions
   need not have "truth makers" that enter into causal relations, I would not say that this
   makes normative relations *irreal*. See *The Domain of Reasons*, pp. 430ff. Saying this
   would seem to suggest that, like fictional characters, they lack some important property that might be claimed for them because they do not correspond to parts of the
   (causal) world.
10. This may be what Derek Parfit has in mind in saying that certain abstract entities exist
    "in a non-ontological sense." See *On What Matters*, Volume Two, pp. 480–3. This slightly
    paradoxical-sounding way of putting the matter may involve identifying ontology with
    a general domain-transcending idea like Quine's idea of ontological commitment. The
    view I am proposing is in a way the reverse of this. I am rejecting this general idea of
    existence and arguing that genuine ontological questions are all domain-specific. I am
    thus endorsing what John Skorupski refers to as "a more radically anti-metaphysical
    view" (*The Domain of Reasons*, pp. 440–1). Although, as I explain in the next paragraph,
    I am not suggesting that (in Skorupski's words) "ontology should be swept away as a
    pseudo-subject," but rather that it should be understood in a domain-specific way.

This move would be mere evasion if there were some general, domain-independent conditions of "existence" such that the various existential claims made in every domain entail or presuppose that entities of the kinds they refer to fulfill these conditions. If this were so, then there would be a genuine external question whether the things to which we are committed actually exist. But there are no such conditions.[11] We make claims expressed by the existential quantifier in many domains, but what is required to justify any existential claim, and what follows from such a claim, varies, depending on the kind of thing that is claimed to exist. The claim that mountains exist is licensed by and licenses certain other claims about the physical world. The claim that there exists a number or set of a certain kind is licensed by and licenses certain other mathematical claims. And in each case that is all there is to it. Nothing more is claimed or required.[12]

To say this is not to deny that there are important and interesting metaphysical or ontological questions. It is only to say that these questions are domain-specific—questions about the metaphysics *of* some particular domain or domains. The metaphysics of a domain in the sense I have in mind is an inquiry into how that domain is best understood at the most abstract and fundamental level. Most traditional metaphysical questions, such as about the nature of time, or of causation, or about whether objects endure or perdure, are questions about the metaphysics of the natural world. There are corresponding questions about other domains, such as whether set theory is basic to all of mathematics. The thesis I will argue for later in this lecture, that the basic element of the normative domain is a relation, *being a reason for*, can be

---

11. Here I agree with Hilary Putnam. See his *Ethics without Ontology*, pp. 94–5, and with William Tait, who states a view about ontology very similar to the one I am advocating in "Truth and Proof: The Platonism of Mathematics." See also Tait's remarks about ontology in his introduction to *The Provenance of Pure Reason*, pp. 6–10.

12. Does this mean that numbers, sets, obligations, and so on, "exist in a different sense," that is to say, that the existential quantifier has a different meaning when it applies to numbers than it has when applied to elephants? I am inclined to say that it does not, but I want to set this question about meaning aside. What I am claiming is (1) that the only thing common to existential claims across all domains is the purely formal logic of the existential quantifier and (2) that the conditions required in order for objects in different domains to exist varies from domain to domain. Whether this variation is fully accounted for by the different sortal terms involved or also reflects variation in the meaning of "exists" is a separate matter on which I take no position. For an argument in favor of the view that "exists" has different senses, see Derek Parfit, *On What Matters*, Volume Two, pp. 469 ff.

seen as a claim about the metaphysics of the normative. These domain-specific metaphysical inquiries can also lead to questions about relations with other domains. For example, a satisfactory account of the normative domain needs to explain the supervenience relations between normative facts and non-normative facts. (I will offer such an explanation later in this lecture.)

There may be good reasons in some cases for limiting our ontology—that is to say, for preferring simpler or more economical theories to more complicated ones. But these reasons are domain-specific. For example, it may be good scientific practice to prefer simpler physical theories. The rationales for preferences of this kind, and what counts as "simplicity" in the relevant senses, will be specific to particular domains, not reflective of a general reason to prefer overall ontological minimalism.

This domain-specific view helps to explain both the appeal and the limits of Gilbert Harman's famous explanatory requirement.[13] In the domain of natural science, the relevant role for entities is in the explanation of natural phenomena. So Harman's explanatory requirement makes good sense in this form: we have reason to be committed to the existence of things of a certain sort in the natural world only if they play a role in explaining what happens in the natural world (including our experience of it). But this maxim is specific to the domain of natural science. It does not apply, as Harman's explanatory requirement is often held to apply, to every domain. It does not apply, for example, to the normative domain, or to mathematics. The relevant maxims for these domains will be, like the version of Harman's requirement that I have just stated, domain-specific. We have reason to quantify over numbers if quantifying over numbers is a good way to formulate this theory. We also have reason to introduce terms denoting new kinds of numbers (such as imaginary and complex numbers) just in case these are useful in providing a more coherent and satisfactory account of the relevant parts of mathematics. And (shifting now from ontology to ideology in Quine's sense) we have reason to introduce additional normative concepts and relations just in case these allow us to give a more coherent and satisfactory account of normative matters.[14] Each of

---

13. Gilbert Harman, *The Nature of Morality*, Chapter 1.
14. In all these domains the task that justifies the introduction of new entities or concepts is the task of describing or explaining the phenomena in question: events in the physical world, or the mathematical or normative facts. Explaining our reactions to,

these requirements makes good sense. But there is no reason to accept Harman's requirement as he formulated it—as a perfectly general requirement applying to all domains—since they do not all aim at the same kinds of understanding (e.g. at the best causal explanations of the world than impinges on our sensory surfaces).

One objection to the view I am recommending might be that it is too permissive. According to this view, it might be said, we could adopt some way of talking which specified criteria of identity for objects of a certain sort, and truth conditions for sentences containing terms referring to them which allowed for existential generalization from such sentences. According to my view, as long as this way of talking was well defined, internally coherent, and *did not have any presuppositions or implications that might conflict with those of other domains, such as science*, by accepting these statements we would be committed to the existence of things quantified over in the existential statements counted as true in this way of talking. They would be among our "ontological commitments." Can we take seriously an idea of existence that comes so cheaply?

My answer is that the question about such entities is not whether they really exist. This question is settled by the standards of the domain, assuming, as I have stipulated, that their existence does not entail implausible claims about other domains, such as the natural world. The question is only whether we have any reason to be concerned with these entities and their properties. Similarly, the indispensability for science of mathematical terms referring to abstract entities such as sets and numbers does not, I would say, provide reason to accept that such

or beliefs about, these facts is a different matter. What I am suggesting as a condition for commitment to the existence of entities of a given type is similar to what Crispin Wright calls "the width of their cosmological role," by which he means "the extent to which citing the kinds of states of affairs with which it deals is potentially contributive to the explanation of things *other than*, or *other than via*, our being in attitudinal states which take such states of affairs as object" (*Truth and Objectivity*, p. 196). The reference to "cosmological" role might suggest that the explanation in question must be causal explanation, of events in the natural world. But Wright goes on to say that this need not be so: "It is not my intention that the Wide Cosmological Role constraint should be satisfiable only by *causally active* states of affairs, nor even that the explanations involved have to be causal. The overarching point, remember, is that there be a *wider range of intelligible and legitimate uses of the relevant state denoters than can be generated merely by the minimal truth aptitude of a discourse*. In principle, therefore, any additional kinds of context featuring the state denoters are significant, and interesting further distinctions may remain to be drawn depending on what the additional kinds of uses are" (*Truth and Objectivity*, p. 198).

things exist. It does not provide reason to believe that they exist as parts of the natural world (they don't) or that they exist within the domain of mathematics (unless it supports mathematical arguments). What this usefulness does is rather to provide reason for scientists to be interested in mathematical entities of this sort and their properties.

Another objection to the view I am proposing is that the idea of existence that it relies on is too "thin" or "minimal." To assess this objection, we need to consider what the relevant notion of "thickness" might amount to. Claims about the existence of objects in the spatio-temporal world do seem to involve a "thick" or "robust" idea of existence. But the "thickness" of these existential claims is provided by the idea of that world itself. For physical objects to exist is for them to have spatio-temporal location, to have various physical properties, and to interact causally with other objects. The relevant idea of "thickness" is thus domain-specific. It is not provided by some further idea of metaphysical reality over and above the properties just mentioned. By the same token, then, the kind of thickness that is relevant to existential statements about numbers is provided by the structure of the relevant mathematical realm. For numbers to exist is for them to stand in various relations with other numbers, such as to be the solution to equations. Similarly, various normative relations give thickness to that domain.

My view is not "minimalist." It aims to give normative and mathematical statements exactly the content and "thickness" that they require when taken literally: no more and certainly no less. But my claim to have done this might be denied. It might be charged that, contrary to what I have maintained, the truth or significance of claims within certain domains requires that the entities they deal with exist in a sense that goes beyond what is directly established by ordinary reasoning within those domains.

In the case of mathematics, the charge would be that in order for mathematical statements to be true, or to have the significance claimed for them, numbers and sets would have to exist in a sense that is not guaranteed by reasoning internal to the mathematical domain (even in the broad sense I emphasized above[15]). In the case of normative truth, the charge would be that in order for normative truths to have the significance normally attributed to them, they would have to be true

15. See p. 20.

(or justified) in a sense that goes beyond what reasoning internal to the normative domain (i.e. thinking about what reasons we have) could by itself establish. I have tried to explain why these charges do not seem to me to have merit in either case.

David Enoch argues that my account of the normative domain is deficient in this way by considering the possibility of people who treat as reasons for action considerations that we would not regard as reasons.[16] He argues that since their reasoning about these "counter-reasons" satisfies the internal standards that they accept, just as our reasoning about reasons satisfies standards internal to the normative domain as we understand it, I am committed to the conclusion that these "counter-reasons" exist just as much as our reasons do, and that my view is therefore unable to give sense to the idea that our conclusions are correct and theirs mistaken.

This problem seems to me illusory. These imagined conclusions about "counter-reasons" conflict with our conclusions about reasons only insofar as they are interpreted as conclusions about reasons. So the question of which of us is correct is a normative question, which can be answered only through normative reasoning. It is a question about the content of the best account of the normative domain—the realm of reasons.[17] To say this is not to say that it is settled by our current beliefs about reasons, or that these beliefs must be correct. Our current substantive conclusions about reasons can be revised in the light of further normative thinking, just as further reasoning about sets can lead us to revise or supplement the axioms of set theory that we currently accept. If we currently believe that certain conclusions about reasons are correct, then we will believe that claims about "counter-reasons" that conflict with these are mistaken. To justify this belief we need to say something about how lines of thinking that lead to those conclusions go wrong. But it adds nothing to say that even if we cannot do this there is nonetheless a further metaphysical fact of the matter about reasons that we are getting right and they are not.[18] I will

---

16. David Enoch, *Taking Morality Seriously*, pp. 122–33.
17. This is the reply Enoch anticipates. *Taking Morality Seriously*, p. 126.
18. A different interpretation of Enoch's thought experiment would hold that what is needed is not a metaphysical notion of normative truth but a practical explanation of why conclusions about reasons have practical authority that conclusions about counter-reasons do not have. I have addressed this worry—that the authority of conclusions about reasons requires justification—in Lecture 1.

return in Lecture 4 to the related question, of why we should believe that questions about reasons for actions have determinate answers, and in what sense these answers are "independent of us."

2. Let me turn now from these general remarks about ontology to some more specific questions about the normative domain. Contrary to what is sometimes said, belief in irreducibly normative truths does not involve commitment to any special entities.[19] The things that can be reasons are not a special kind of entity but ordinary facts, in many cases facts about the natural world. For example, the fact that the edge of a piece of metal is sharp is a reason for me, now, not to press my hand against it.[20]

The distinctive aspect of normative truths is not the things that are reasons but the normative relations, such as being a reason for something, or being a sufficient or conclusive reason. What is special about normative claims is thus not a matter of ontology *in Quine's sense* (the things quantified over), but rather of what Quine called "ideology" (the predicates employed).

The relation I will be concerned with in this lecture is the relation of simply counting in favor of some action or attitude. Something can be a reason in this relatively weak sense without being a decisive or conclusive reason. I will discuss these stronger reason relations in Lecture 5.

Whether a certain fact is a reason, and what it is a reason for, depends on an agent's circumstances. The fact that this piece of metal is sharp is a reason for me not to press my hand against it, but under different circumstances it might be a reason *to* press my hand against it, and

---

19. As I have argued above, even if reasons were best understood as entities, that is as things quantified over, this would not mean that the normative domain had external ontological commitments than one might find troubling. The question whether reasons are, at the most fundamental normative level, a special kind of normative element or rather elements of some other kind that enter into normative relations is a question internal to the normative domain, about how that domain is best understood—a question within what I called above the metaphysics *of* the normative domain. I am grateful to Markus Willaschek for helpful discussion of this issue.

20. As just indicated, I take it that the things that are reasons—that figure in the first place of the relation R—are facts. In order to avoid cumbersome locutions, however, I will use "*p*" ambiguously, sometimes to refer to a fact, sometimes as a sentential variable replaceable by the content of a fact. The context should make clear which of these is intended. This solution is not entirely satisfactory, but I believe that nothing of substance turns on it. I thank Tyler Burge for pressing me on this point, and Selim Berker for helpful advice.

under still different circumstances a reason to do something else, such as to put it into the picnic basket if I will later have reason to want to cut cheese. This suggests that "is a reason for" is a four-place relation, $R(p, x, c, a)$, holding between a fact p, an agent x, a set of conditions c, and an action or attitude a. This is the relation that holds just in case p is a reason for a person x in situation c to do or hold a.[21]

We should bear in mind, however, that the items that figure in the four places of this relation are often interrelated. To begin with, what goes in the a place is an action that x does, or an attitude x holds. This is, however, built into the relation R itself, so that what occupies the fourth place in the relation is an action or attitude type, specified without reference to x, and R holds just in case p is a reason for x to do an action, or hold an attitude, of this type under the relevant circumstances.

Things are more complicated with respect to p and c. A person, x, might have reason for doing a because it is necessary to save her child's life. In this case p is what Thomas Nagel called a subjective reason, one that involves essential reference to the agent.[22] It follows from the fact that a would save the life of x's child that doing a would save *someone's* life, and this fact, p', would be a reason for another person, y, to do a. This would be what Nagel called an objective, or later, an agent-neutral reason.[23] The point is just that the kind of normative claim made by a claim that $R(p, x, c, a)$ may vary depending on the way in which p is or is not related to the agent, x.[24]

21. I will consider other, stronger normative relations in Lecture 5. The relational character of claims about reasons has been noted by others, including Jonathan Dancy, Terence Cuneo, and John Skorupski. See Dancy, *Ethics Without Principles*, Chapter 3, especially pp. 38ff; Cuneo, *The Normative Web*, p. 65; and Skorupski, *The Domain of Reasons*, Chapter 2. Cuneo seems to have in mind a three-place relation (or perhaps a four-place one including a place for the agent). Dancy mentions two two-place relations: the favoring/disfavoring relation and the enabling/disenabling relation. A consideration can be a disabler if its presence undermines what otherwise would be a consideration favoring an action, but does not itself favor or disfavor that action. As will be clear below, and in Lecture 5, my four-place relation $R(p, x, c, a)$ is intended to encompass both of these relations. Considerations c that are required in order for $R(p, x, c, a)$ to hold are enablers in Dancy's sense. Skorupski considers a six-place relation, involving places for time and the degree of strength of the reason. He also distinguishes the simple relation of some fact's being a specific reason (of a certain strength), and the idea of an agent's overall reasons for something, and the idea of an agent's having sufficient reason for something. See *The Domain of Reasons*, pp. 36–44.
22. Nagel, *The Possibility of Altruism*, p. 90.
23. *The Possibility of Altruism*, p. 90; *The View from Nowhere*, pp. 138–9, 152–3.
24. I thank Toni Rønnow-Rasmussen for urging me to explain how this is the case.

The circumstances c in which something is a reason may also involve reference to the agent. The fact that p may be a reason for x to do a only because x is in a certain institutional position, such as a citizen of a certain country, or member of a committee, in virtue of which x is eligible to do a. The possibility of such interrelations between $p, x, c,$ and a is not a problem for the account I am offering, but rather a complexity that it allows for, which should be borne in mind.

It should also be noted that, although the facts that are reasons are often natural facts, normative facts can also be reasons. So, for example, the fact that a law would be unjust may be a reason for me to vote against it if I am in a position to do so. Similarly, the circumstances, c, under which a certain fact is claimed to be a reason may be specified in normative terms. So, for example, we might say that the fact that jumping out of the window is the only way to save a person's life is a reason for that person to jump because she is in circumstances in which she has reason to go on living. Alternatively, these circumstances may be alluded to only in an unspecific way, such as by saying simply that *in her present circumstances* the fact that jumping out the window is the only way to save her life is a reason for her to jump, and leaving it open for further specification exactly what these circumstances (non-normatively specified) must be like in order for this to be the case.[25] Our claims about reasons for action are very often vague in this way about the exact circumstances under which we are claiming something to be a reason. Much of the process of thinking about what reasons we have, and trying to make our beliefs about reasons consistent, involves working out what these conditions are.

A final thing that should be noted is the factive character of most statements about reasons: p is not a reason for someone in c to do a unless p obtains and the person in question is actually in circumstances c. As will become clear below, this is important in understanding the relation between normative and non-normative claims.

My characterization of this basic normative relation is intended to be non-committal on important normative issues. It is consistent, for example, with the view that the reasons an agent has depend on his or her desires, because it leaves open whether c must contain facts about the agent's desires. Also, it is an implication of my view that something is a reason for an agent only if it is also a reason for any other agent in

---

25. I will return to this issue in Lecture 5.

similar circumstances. But the view leaves open what counts as "similar." In particular, it leaves open whether the relevant features of these circumstances are always finitely specifiable in non-normative terms.[26]

3. Even if the idea of irreducibly normative truths does not have troubling ontological implications, other potential difficulties remain having to do with the relation between normative facts and natural facts. Normative claims are not—as may be the case with claims about sets—simply about a special distinct realm. These claims are in an important sense *about* the natural world: they attribute normative significance to natural facts, such as the sharpness of a piece of metal. The relation R seems, therefore, to correspond to a normative relational *property* that holds between things in the natural world, and it may be wondered what this relational property is.

Also, normative truths are distinct from (not entailed by) non-normative truths, but they are linked to non-normative truths in two significant ways: they vary when naturalistic facts vary, and, it is said, they do not vary as long as the naturalistic facts remain the same. These relations of covariance and supervenience need to be explained. To address these questions, it will be helpful to begin by looking more closely at the relation between the normative and the non-normative.

It is widely believed, by both cognitivists and non-cognitivists about the normative, that there is an important distinction, sometimes called an "unbridgeable gap," between normative and non-normative judgments—between "values" and "facts," as it is often put. This idea is naturally expressed as the thesis that no normative statement can be derived from any consistent set of non-normative statements via logic and conceptual entailments. But this formulation needs to be clarified by specifying the kind of derivation that is in question and characterizing more clearly the classes of statements on either side of the "gap."

As Hilary Putnam has observed, claims about the gap between facts and values have generally taken as their starting point some characterization of the class of non-normative statements, with which value judgments are then contrasted.[27] For Hume, "is" statements were

---

26. This is one point at issue between particularists and others. See Dancy, *Ethics Without Principles*, pp. 80–1. Dancy states the point as one about specifying *morally* relevant features, but I take it to be one that applies also to claims about reasons more generally. I will return to this question in Lecture 5.

27. Putnam, *The Collapse of the Fact/Value Dichotomy*, pp. 19–24.

identified with "relations of ideas" and "matters of fact." For the logical positivists, the relevant class consisted of analytic statements and those that are empirically verifiable. I will start on the other side, beginning with the class of normative statements.

The characterization of the normative domain is, however, a matter of controversy. I am inclined to hold that normative statements are statements involving claims about the reasons that people have. My working hypothesis is that other concepts normally regarded as normative, such as good, value, and moral right and wrong, are best understood in terms of reasons, or at least that judgments involving these concepts are best understood in terms of claims about reasons insofar as these judgments are genuinely normative—that is to say, not interpretable in physical, psychological, or social terms that are clearly non-normative.[28] This thesis is controversial.[29] I will, however, generally assume it in what follows: when I speak of "the normative domain" I will have in mind the domain of judgments about reasons. Most of what I will go on to say in these lectures will not depend on this, but I will note those places at which it may make a difference.

It is, however, not satisfactory to understand the fact/value distinction as a distinction between the domain of statements making non-trivial claims about the reasons people have and the domain of statements not making such claims. One problem with this was noted by A. N. Prior.[30] Let F be a statement agreed to be non-normative, and N any statement agreed to be normative. What, then, about F v N? It follows logically from F. So if no normative judgment can follow from a non-normative one then it must be non-normative. But from F v N and not-F one can deduce N. So F v N cannot be non-normative if the thesis of non-derivability holds.

We can avoid this difficulty by stating the thesis that there is a fact/value distinction as the thesis that no claim that $R(p, x, c, a)$ is derivable from any consistent set of non-normative statements. But if derivability means logical entailment, and non-normative statements are just those statements without non-trivial occurrences of the relation R,

---

28. For my views on goodness and on moral right and wrong see, respectively, Chapter 2 and Chapter 4 of *What We Owe to Each Other*.

29. For an alternative account, taking attributive goodness as the fundamental normative concept, see Judith Thomson, *Normativity*. For my response to Thomson, see "The Unity of the Normative."

30. In "The Autonomy of Ethics."

then this thesis is just an instance of the general logical point that, for any predicate G, a statement of the form G(a) is not entailed by any consistent set of statements not containing G. This says nothing in particular about normative statements and their relation to the non-normative.

One way in which the thesis can be strengthened is by expanding the relevant notion of derivability to include not only logical entailment but also conceptual entailment. This yields the thesis that no claim that $R(p, x, c, a)$ holds, or does not hold, can be derived via logical and conceptual entailment from any consistent set of non-normative statements. So understood, the thesis rules out analytic naturalism, which holds that claims about reasons can be analyzed in non-normative terms. But insofar as non-normative statements are still understood to be statements not involving the relation R, this thesis goes farther than most understandings of the fact/value distinction by building in the idea that the concept of a reason is fundamental to the normative domain, and cannot be analyzed in *any* other terms, normative or non-normative.

To obtain a more plausible interpretation of the idea that there is an important distinction between normative statements and non-normative ones we need to give a more specific characterization of the class of non-normative statements. So, for example, we may say that no claim that $R(p, x, c, a)$ holds or does not hold can be derived via logical and conceptual entailment from any consistent set of physical and psychological claims. It may, however, be questioned whether all physical and psychological claims are truly non-normative. It is sometimes pointed out, for example, that the justification for scientific conclusions, often involves appeal to what are clearly values, such as simplicity, clarity, and the like. As Hilary Putnam has put it, "epistemic values are also values."[31] This seems to me quite true, but not in conflict with the thesis I am now proposing.

The claim that we have reason to believe a particular empirical proposition is a normative claim. This is so even if the reasons cited are purely epistemic: considerations that indicate that the proposition in question is true. Beyond this, our reasons for accepting a scientific theory may, or may not, be based on further reasons that

31. See Putnam, *The Collapse of the Fact/Value Dichotomy*, pp. 135–45.

are not all truth-related.[32] But neither of these possibilities indicates a puzzling intermingling of facts and values. If they appear to do so this is due to a failure to distinguish between the claim that we have sufficient reason for accepting a theory, or for counting a proposition as true, and the claims made by that theory or proposition. The former may be normative even when the latter are not.[33]

Questions might also be raised about the normativity of psychology. No doubt some psychological categories are normative in the sense of involving *norms*, i.e. standards.[34] ("Believer" and "rational being," for example, may well be normative in this sense.) I would argue that these categories are not normative in the sense of involving claims about the reasons that an agent has, which is my present concern. But I will not enter into these matters here.

Another apparent difficulty for the thesis of non-derivability of normative statements from non-normative ones as I have stated it arises from the factive character of most claims about reasons: p cannot be a reason for anything unless it is the case that p. So it would seem to follow from the non-normative claim that p does not obtain that the normative claim that $R(p, x, c, a)$ also does not hold. This might seem to be a case of inferring a normative conclusion from purely non-normative premises. It might be questioned in what sense this "follows." It does not seem to be a case of logical entailment, nor, I would say, is it best characterized as a matter of conceptual truth. This is a question to which I will return.

Assuming that if p does not obtain it follows, in the relevant sense, that $R(p, x, c, a)$ does not hold, we might rule out such counterexamples by taking the claim of non-derivability to be that no *positive* atomic statement of the form $R(p, x, c, a)$ follows via logical and conceptual entailment from any consistent set of physical and psychological statements. This move might avoid the problem, but it also ignores an important point about the relation R, which is that the essentially normative content of a statement that $R(p, x, c, a)$ is independent of whether p holds. This normative content lies in the claim that, whether p obtains or not, *should* p hold then it is a reason for

---

32. For discussion, see Joseph Raz, "Reasons: Practical and Adaptive."

33. A point made by Allan Gibbard. See *Wise Choices, Apt Feelings*, p. 34.

34. See Tyler Burge, *Origins of Objectivity*, pp. 311 ff.

someone in c to do a. So I will take what I will call a *pure normative claim* to be a claim that R(p, x, c, a) holds (or does not hold), under-stood in this way.[35]

Most of the claims we commonly think of as normative are not pure normative claims, but *mixed normative claims*. They involve pure normative claims but also make or presuppose claims about natural facts. This is familiar in the case of what are commonly called "thick ethical concepts," such as "cruel," the application of which involves claims about reasons in a variety of ways.[36]

To claim that Caligula was cruel is certainly to make a claim about what he *saw* as a reason and responded to in his actions, and what, on the other hand, he was generally indifferent to. Such claims attribute normative views to Caligula, but do not make any such claims themselves. So far at least, the claims are purely psy-chological. But genuinely normative elements may enter in two related ways.

One normative element enters insofar as the charge of cruelty involves not only the claim that Caligula was indifferent to certain concerns, such as the suffering of his victims, but also the claim that these were things that he should not have been indifferent to, because they really are reasons. A further normative element lies in the idea that cruelty is something one has reason to avoid in oneself and to condemn in others, and more generally, that one has good reason to react differently to someone who is cruel than to someone who is not—to avoid their company, not to trust them in certain contexts, and so on. These two elements are related. The reasons one has to respond differently to someone who is cruel depend on the particular reasons that a cruel person is insensitive to, and the importance of responding correctly to these reasons.

These normative elements are central to the concept of cruelty. They give the concept its point and guide its empirical content. A person who did not understand these normative elements could not grasp the concept and tell which psychological traits and forms of

---

35. I believe that such claims are examples of what Kit Fine calls "world-bound norma-tive conditionals" in "The Varieties of Necessity," pp. 272–3.

36. The term "thick ethical concepts" was introduced by Bernard Williams. See *Ethics and the Limits of Philosophy*, pp. 129–31, 141–2. Hilary Putnam mentions cruel as a coun-terexample to the idea that there is "an absolute fact/value *dichotomy*." *The Collapse of the Fact/Value Dichotomy*, p. 35.

behavior count as cruel.[37] But one need not take examples as complex as these to find mixed normative claims. Even claims involving "thin" ethical concepts such as "morally wrong" are mixed normative claims in my view: to claim that an action is morally wrong is to claim that it has properties that provide reasons to reject any principle that would permit it. In everyday English, even the claim, "She has a good reason not to do it, since it would hurt her sister's feelings" is a mixed claim, since it cannot be true unless the action in question would in fact hurt her sister's feelings.

So in my view, the domain of normative statements is quite diverse. It includes, in addition to pure normative claims, mixed normative claims of a variety of sorts, including but not limited to, claims involving "thick ethical concepts." These claims involve or presuppose non-normative claims in a variety of complex ways.[38] The essential truth in the fact/value distinction lies in the role and status of pure normative claims, as I will now explain.

4. Attending to the difference between pure normative claims and mixed normative claims helps to explain a number of things about the relation between the normative and the non-normative that otherwise seem puzzling.

The idea that there is a "logical gap" between normative and non-normative claims can seem puzzling, because we commonly make what may seem to be sound inferences from non-normative facts to normative conclusions. For example, from

---

37. I thus agree with Williams (*Ethics and the Limits of* Philosophy, pp. 141–2) that judgments involving thick ethical concepts cannot be analyzed into a "descriptive" (non-normative) part and a normative attitude that is then attached to this. As I have said, the non-normative content of think ethical concepts depends on the normative content of these concepts in complex ways. But for this very reason I would not agree with Williams that the non-normative content of claims involving thick concepts (or other mixed normative statements) makes them "world-guided" in a sense that confers greater objectivity than pure normative statements enjoy. The non-normative content of such statements is itself normatively "guided." Williams' thesis of non-disentanglement thus undermines his suggestion that judgments employing these concepts have special objectivity. This may seem to be the case only because those who use the concepts have a high level of agreement on these underlying normative judgments.

38. This diversity may well be what Putnam has in mind in saying that the fact/value distinction is a distinction, not a dichotomy. Unlike a dichotomy, a distinction, in the sense he has in mind, need not be omnipresent: it need not be the case that every item of the relevant kind falls on one side or the other.

(1) If Jones does not leave the burning building now, he will be killed

it seems to follow that

(2) Jones has a reason to leave the burning building now.

If there is a logical gap between the normative and the non-normative, how can it be that we leap over this gap with ease all the time?

The answer is that although (2) is not entailed (logically or conceptually) by (1) it nonetheless "follows from" (1) with the aid of

(3) Jones's situation is such that the fact that doing a is necessary for him to avoid dying now is a reason for him to do a.

(3) is still a mixed normative claim insofar as it involves a claim about what Jones' situation actually is. But we could put these conditions c, whatever they are (facts about Jones' life in virtue of which he has reason to want to go on living) into the earlier premises, and then restate (3) as a pure normative claim that anyone in these circumstances has reason to do what is necessary to prolong his life.

To say that (2) follows from (1) with the aid of (3), and, ultimately, with the aid of a pure normative version of (3), is not to say that anyone who makes this move must employ (3) as a premise. As I will explain further in Lecture 3, a rational person who accepts (3) will simply *see* (1) as a reason for Jones to leave the building now. Nonetheless, it would be appropriate for such a person to cite (3) as an explanation of her move from (1) to (2) if this move is challenged. It is therefore somewhat misleading to say that the move from (1) to (2) is a move from the non-normative to the normative, since this move is made "with the aid of" a pure normative claim (or, to put it another way, since the validity of this move is a normative matter). When we see that the role of pure normative claims is precisely to license such moves, it is no longer surprising that we cannot "get from" a normative claim to a non-normative one without "already making" a normative claim. This also answers the question I raised earlier about the sense in which it "follows from" the falsity of p that $R(p, x, c, a)$ does not hold. The connection between these is not logical or conceptual entailment. Rather, it is simply a normative truth that if p is not the case then neither is it the case that $R(p, x, c, a)$.

Mixed normative claims, such as (2), thus depend on non-normative claims, this dependence being determined, ultimately, by pure normative claims. It might be tempting to say that mixed normative claims such as (2) are "true in virtue of" non-normative claims such as (1). But this would be misleading insofar as it suggested that they are true only in virtue of the truth of these claims, neglecting the role of pure normative claims in determining how this is the case.

Pure normative claims do not depend on non-normative claims at all. Any such dependence has been subjunctivized away through the process described above. It is therefore not possible to move *from* non-normative claims *to* pure normative claims in a way analogous to the move from (1) to (2).

The phenomena of covariance and supervenience, which many have found puzzling, are also explained by distinguishing clearly between pure and mixed normative claims. Indeed, what I will say about these phenomena will just be a metaphysical version of the points I have just made about ordinary reasoning.

The problem is to explain why it is the case, if normative truths are not logically or conceptually tied to non-normative truths, that most normative facts nonetheless vary as non-normative facts vary, and cannot vary when non-normative facts do not vary. To understand these phenomena it is important to be clear what kind of normative claims are in question. The normative facts that can vary as non-normative facts vary are facts that consist in the truth of mixed normative claims, such as the claim that someone has a reason to do a certain action, or that a particular consideration is such a reason. So, for example, the fact that it would be very painful to put my hand into a flame is a reason not to do so. But if putting one's hand into a flame were not painful, then "the fact that it would be very painful to put my hand in to a flame" would not be a fact, and I would not have the reason just mentioned. So mixed normative facts depend on non-normative facts, and *which* non-normative facts they depend on is a normative matter, determined by the truth of pure normative claims.[39] The truth of pure

---

39. If this is correct, then it seems to follow that the dependence of the normative on the non-normative is quite different from the dependence of the mental on the physical. Normative judgments make claims about (the normative significance of) non-normative facts. That mixed normative facts co-vary with non-normative facts, and the particular facts on which they depend, is determined by pure normative truths, and it is also a normative matter that pure normative truths do not vary "on their own." By contrast, it is not part of the *content* of claims about mental phenomena that they attribute mental properties to physical states, and "mentalistic" truths do not specify which physical states mental states depend on and co-vary with. Confidence that the

normative claims, by contrast, does not depend on, or co-vary with, non-normative facts.

Nor do pure normative facts vary "on their own." Given that they do not, the mixed normative facts that depend on them supervene on non-normative facts. This again is a normative matter, a case of normative necessity.[40] This seems evident from reflection on what pure normative truths are.[41] But it does not seem to me, on reflection, to be something that we should find puzzling. Given that pure normative facts are not contingent in the most obvious way—that is, dependent on contingent facts about the natural world—why should we expect them to be contingent in some further sense?

These two parallel features of the relation between the normative and the non-normative—the appearance of a gap that we nonetheless cross without difficulty and the phenomena of covariance and supervenience without logical or conceptual entailment—are more likely to seem puzzling if, in considering the normative side of the distinction, one focuses on normative claims the relational character of which is not apparent, such as claims that something is good or that some action is morally wrong. These claims appear simply to assign to their subject some normative property, so the question arises about the relation between having this property and having various natural properties. I have argued that the relation between the normative and the non-normative is clearer when we focus instead on pure normative

mental co-varies with the physical and cannot vary independently arises rather from the acceptance of what might be called the hegemony of the physical: the thesis that all natural phenomena have physical explanations. As Kit Fine has pointed out to me, the relation between the normative and the non-normative is more like the relation between the mathematical and the physical: "mixed" mathematical facts vary with non-mathematical facts; the particular facts they vary with being determined by pure mathematical facts, which do not themselves vary at all.

40. Kit Fine argues, in "The Varieties of Necessity," that the necessity of (some) normative claims is distinct from and not reducible to metaphysical necessity. I believe the necessity of pure normative facts is an instance of normative necessity of the kind he has in mind.

41. Simon Blackburn appears to agree. He writes, "A quasi-realist will see both covariance and the asymmetry of dependency as a reflection of the fact that valuing is *to be done* in the light of an object's natural properties, and without that constraint nothing recognizably ethical could be approached at all" ("Supervenience Revisited," p. 146). But Blackburn did say earlier (in "Moral Realism," p. 116) that if someone claimed that two actions were the same in every respect except that one was much worse (I take it he means morally) this "would be a logical and not merely a moral mistake that had been made," and that if this kind of variation were merely a moral impossibility then "moral worth would not supervene on naturalistic properties in my sense." He and I agree if his remark in "Supervenience Revisited" revises this earlier view.

claims, which have exactly the function of assigning normative significance to non-normative facts.

Although I have stated this explanation of the relation between the normative and the non-normative in terms of the relation of being a reason for someone to do something, this does not mean that my explanation depends on the more controversial hypothesis that that relation is the fundamental normative notion, in terms of which all other genuinely normative notions can be analyzed. If the relation R, and other reason relations, are not the fundamental normative notions in this sense, then there can be pure normative claims of other kinds, which may or may not be analyzable in terms of reasons. For example, instead of focusing on the one-place predicate "x is good" and the corresponding one-place property, consider the relation "having property p contributes to a thing x's being good" or "having property p contributes to a thing x's being a good y." Using these relations we can formulate pure normative claims about goodness, which, like the pure normative claims I have been discussing that involve R, are normatively necessary and have the function of assigning normative significance to non-normative properties. The same could be said about the moral property "x is morally wrong" and the relation, "an action x with property p, done in circumstances c, is wrong." The important point is not about the fundamentality of reasons but about the central role of pure normative claims, whatever normative concepts they involve.[42]

5. I turn now to the question of normative properties. Many who accept the idea that normative concepts are non-natural maintain that it would be odd to think that there are normative properties—features "of the world"—corresponding to these concepts. Allan Gibbard and Mark Schroeder, for example, agree that normative concepts cannot be analyzed in naturalistic terms, but they maintain, in different ways, that the properties signified by normative terms are naturalistic.[43] So I need to consider the relation between concepts and properties, and how normative properties should be understood.

---

42. I am grateful to Stavroula Tsinorema for a question that prompted me to recognize this fact.

43. In different ways because Schroeder is a reductive naturalist while Gibbard is an expressivist. I will discuss their views more fully below.

In one sense, the distinction between concepts and properties is clear. Identifying concepts is a matter of determining the content of our thoughts. Specifying properties is a matter of determining the nature of things in the world to which those concepts correspond. The question is when and how the characterization of the property corresponding to a concept will go beyond what is specified by that concept itself. In some cases, having the property signified by a concept is just a matter of having those features included in the concept. So if one understands the concept, then there is no more to be said about the property. In other cases, however, there is more to be said about what it is to be a thing in the world of the kind to which the concept applies. The interesting question is when and why this is the case.

Consider first a concept of a natural kind, such as water. If the concept, *water*, is defined only by features of water that figure in our everyday experience, such as "colorless liquid that falls as rain and fills rivers, streams, lakes and oceans," then there is more to be said about what water is: for example, that it has the chemical composition, H_2O. We might say, then, that the property of being water is a matter of having those physical characteristics, whatever they may be, that are responsible for the observed characteristics that figure in the concept. Something similar might be said about other concepts of natural kinds, such as the concept of lightning. In all these cases, the fact that there may be more to the property signified by a concept than is specified in that concept is simply a reflection of the fact that the concepts in question identify *natural* phenomena on the basis of certain features that are apparent to us. This leaves open the possibility that there is more to be said about the nature of these phenomena—that is to say about what in the world described by chemistry and physics is responsible for these features.

There may be a broad parallel in the case of some normative concepts. The concept, morally wrong, for example, includes such marks as being "an action that anyone has very strong reason not to perform, and which makes appropriate guilt on the part of one who has done it and resentment on the part of those to whom it is done." But this leaves open what reason there is not to perform these actions, and to feel guilt or resentment as a result of their being done. A person can understand and employ the concept *morally wrong* without having a very clear idea what these reasons are, just as someone can have the concept, *water*, without knowing the chemical composition of water.

There is more to be said about what makes something morally wrong, and the task of giving this further account might be said to be the task of characterizing the property of moral wrongness.[44] If this is right, then this is another case in which the minimal understanding of a property is insufficient. The further characterization of a natural kind such as water is scientific—a matter of chemistry and physics. The further explanation of moral wrongness is normative—a matter of identifying the relevant reasons.

My concern in this lecture is with the concept of a reason—more exactly, the relational concept $R(p, x, c, a)$. So the question before us is whether there is something further to be said about what it is to be a reason, beyond what is given just by this relational concept, something further that might be said to identify the property signified by that concept. Since the concept of a reason, like that of moral wrongness, is a normative concept, it would seem that this further explanation would also need to be normative.

If the concept of a reason is that of a consideration that "counts in favor of" something for an agent in certain circumstances, the further explanation might be an explanation of what "counting in favor of" amounts to. This might take the form of an explanation of the "grip" or "authority" of reasons, of the kind offered by Kantians and others, who believe that the authority of reasons can be grounded in an idea of rationality. If successful, such an account of the property of being a reason would have the right kind of explanatory role—a normative explanatory role analogous to the physical explanatory role of the property of being water.

As I have said, however, it seems to me that no such further explanation of reasons need or can be given: the "grip" that a consideration that is a reason has on a person for whom it is a reason is just being a reason for him or her. This is the position I referred to in Lecture 1 as "reasons fundamentalism." I will have more to say in later lectures about the appeal of Kantian and other rationality-based alternatives to this position. Here I want to consider a different alternative view, which maintains that an account of the property of being a reason can and should be naturalistic.

---

44. I took this line in *What We Owe to Each Other* (see p. 12). Derek Parfit criticized it in "Justifiability to Each Other." For further discussion, see my "Wrongness and Reasons: A Reexamination," and Parfit, *On What Matters*, Volume 1, pp. 368–70.

Allan Gibbard, for example, accepts the idea that there are normative concepts, but objects to the idea that there are normative properties, which he believes would be metaphysically odd.[45] It may be that he would not object to the idea of normative properties in the minimal sense I have proposed.[46] Gibbard does not object to the idea of normative facts in a similarly minimal sense. He writes that if by "facts" we mean simply "true thoughts," then there are normative facts. If there "is no more to claiming 'It's true that pain is bad' than to claim that pain is bad; the fact that pain is bad just consists in pain's being bad; [and] to believe that pain is bad is just to accept that it is," "Then it's true that pain is bad and it's a fact that pain is bad."[47]

Gibbard's positive proposal is to construct the property that constitutes a normative concept out of the natural properties in virtue of which things fall under that normative concept in various possible situations. If, for example, P_1 is the thing to do in C_1, P_2 is the thing to do in C_2, and so on, then the property that constitutes the normative concept "being the thing to do" is the property of having the property P_1 in C_1, or having the property P_2 in C_2, and so on.[48] This "grand property" is related to the normative concept "thing to do" in some of the ways that one might expect to hold between a property and the corresponding concept. The two are, for example, necessarily coextensive, but their being coextensive is not a priori. Nonetheless, a grand property constructed in this way does not seem to me a plausible candidate to be the property corresponding to a normative concept because it does not explain the main features of things picked out by that concept, in the way in which having the chemical composition H_2O explains the features of water, and the way in which a Kantian account seeks to explain the authority of reasons. To put the point in Moorean terms, in the case of *good* the grand property Gibbard constructs would be closer to an account of what things are good than to an account of what *good* is.

---

45. *Thinking How to Live*, pp. 29–34.
46. Simon Blackburn accepts the idea of normative properties in this sense. He writes, "There is no harm in saying that ethical predicates refer to properties, when such properties are merely the semantic shadows of the fact that they function as predicates" ("How to be an Ethical Anti-Realist," p. 181).
47. *Thinking How to Live*, pp. 182–3.
48. *Thinking How to Live*, Chapter 5, esp. pp. 98–9.

In this respect there is more to be said for the naturalistic account of the property of being a reason offered by Mark Schroeder. Like Gibbard, Schroeder agrees that the concept of a reason cannot be analyzed in non-normative terms.[49] But he believes that the property of being a reason can be so analyzed. Specifically, he believes that for p to be a reason for a person x in situation c to do a is for there to be some q such that x has a desire whose object is q and the truth of p is part of what explains how x's doing a promotes q.[50]

This account of what it is to be a reason is stated in purely naturalistic terms. So it may seem doomed at the start. To identify being a reason with a naturalistic property seems immediately to destroy its normativity. Schroeder's response is that if normativity is best understood in terms of reasons (as I would agree), then his account preserves normativity as long as it captures the idea of a reason.[51] One may think (as I do) that the naturalistic character of his account prevents it from doing this. But beyond merely asserting that his account cannot preserve the normative character of reasons, we should consider the grounds Schroeder offers for believing that it does.

What would be required in order for this analysis to be successful? First, there would have to be a reasonably good extensional fit with our firmest intuitive judgments about reasons.[52] This is not sufficient, however. The account proposed above following Gibbard's model, for example, would meet this condition. But it seemed a poor candidate to be the property of being a reason in part because it did nothing to explain the features that reasons have. Schroeder believes that his account does just this. Specifically, he believes that it explains why someone is motivated by the belief that he or she has a reason to do something, explains why facts about reasons supervene on natural facts, and explains why the reasons that some people have differ from the reasons that others have.

I agree that Schroeder's account offers explanations of the first two kinds, although I believe that a non-reductive account can provide

---

49. *Slaves of the Passions*, p. 65.
50. *Slaves of the Passions*, p. 59. I have modified Schroeder's definition slightly to fit my statement of R(p, x, c, a). One apparent difference, which I will set aside for the moment, is that his definition, on the face of it, applies only to reasons for action.
51. *Slaves of the Passions*, pp. 79ff.
52. Schroeder argues, in Chapters 5 and 6 of *Slaves of the Passions*, that his account meets this condition. I do not find those arguments persuasive, but I will leave this disagreement aside.

explanations that are equally good, if not better. I have already explained what a non-reductive account has to say about covariance and supervenience, and I will return to the question of motivation in a later lecture. So I will focus here on the third claim.

Schroeder's main example, which he returns to throughout the book, involves two people, Ronnie and Bradley. Both have been invited to a party where there will be dancing. "But," Schroeder says, "While Ronnie loves to dance, Bradley can't stand it." He claims, plausibly, that the fact that there will be dancing at the party is a reason for Ronnie to go to the party but not a reason for Bradley to go. Moreover, it seems uncontroversial that this difference between Ronnie's reasons and Bradley's is explained by "some feature of their psychologies." The Humean Theory of Reasons, as Schroeder understands it, is that "Every reason is explained by the kind of psychological state that explains Ronnie's reason in the same way as Ronnie's is."[53] (Schroeder sees his own view as one particular version of The Humean Theory.)

If what is to be explained is the difference between Ronnie's reasons and Bradley's, then it does seem uncontroversial that this difference lies in something about their psychologies. But this claim is more controversial if what is in question is the (most fundamental) explanation of Ronnie's reason to go to the dance. It is very plausible to say that what explains the difference between Ronnie's reasons and Bradley's is the fact that Ronnie enjoys dancing and Bradley does not.[54] But this leaves open the question of why the fact that Ronnie enjoys dancing makes it the case that the fact that there will be dancing at the party gives him a reason to go. This might be, as Humean theories hold, because Ronnie has a desire for experiences that he finds pleasant. Or it might be, as many non-Humean theories would maintain, simply because (in most cases) the fact that a person would find doing something pleasant is a reason for him or her to do it.[55] So, although it

---

53. *Slaves of the Passions*, p. 2.
54. Schroeder considers this possibility as one candidate for the psychological feature that, according to a Humean Theory, explains Ronnie's reason, hence as one possible variant of a Humean view (*Slaves of the Passions*, p. 3). What I am suggesting is that this explanation of Ronnie's reason could be offered by a non-Humean theory, and that this possibility undermines the support that the example of Ronnie and Bradley offers for a Humean theory.
55. There is also a question here about time. Is the psychological state that explains Ronnie's reason a state that he is in at the time he is deciding whether to go to the party, such as the fact that he wants to dance at that later time, or a desire for experiences

may be non-controversial that what explains the difference between Ronnie's reasons and Bradley's is something about their psychological states, it is controversial whether the most fundamental explanation of Ronnie's reason is a psychological state. Indeed, this is just the point at issue between Humeans and non-Humeans.

The possibility of a hedonistic explanation of Ronnie's reason for going to the dance comes up at two further points in Schroeder's argument. The first is in his interesting discussion of what he calls the "no background conditions view." This is the view that any condition that is needed in a full explanation of why something is a reason for a person to perform a given action must itself be part of that reason.[56] If this view were correct, then on a Humean theory a full statement of every reason for action would make reference to the agent's desires. This would, Schroeder says, give all reasons an implausible self-regarding character, suggesting that all agents are ultimately moved only by the satisfaction of their own desires. Since not all reasons seem to have this self-regarding character, this would count against the plausibility of Humean theories.

Schroeder's response is to argue that not every factor that is needed to explain why a certain consideration is a reason for an agent is also part of that reason. "If Ronnie genuinely desires to dance, then *all it should take* for him to be moved to go to the party is the thought that there will be dancing there."[57] There is no need for him to think also "and I desire to dance." This general point, about the distinction between reasons and background conditions, is quite correct, and important. It is recognized in my formulation of the relation "being a reason for" by the distinction between p, which is the agent's reason for a, and those features, c, of the agent's situation in virtue of which p is a reason. But the application of this distinction to the case of Ronnie and Bradley seems to count against Schroeder's view rather than to support it.

In general, including "and I desire X" in the content of a reason gives the agent's action an *implausible* self-regarding character because in many cases the agent desires the thing in question for some reason

that, at the time of their occurrence, he will find enjoyable? Or is the fact that he has reason to go to the dance explained by a future psychological state, the pleasure that (he has good reason to expect) he will feel when dancing at the party?

56. *Slaves of the Passions*, p. 23.
57. *Slaves of the Passions*, p. 27.

not connected with the satisfaction of his or her desires. If a person desires to contribute to the alleviation of world poverty, it is implausible to say that part of her reason for sending a check is that this will fulfill her desire. But if Ronnie goes to the party because he likes to dance, then his reason for going is most plausibly understood as having a self-regarding character that it would not have if, for example, he desired to go to the dance because he had promised to take his girlfriend dancing (even though he did not much enjoy it himself), or if he desired to go, and to dance, because he wanted to encourage his younger siblings' interest in dancing, in order to keep them from more dangerous pursuits. In cases of the latter kinds, including, as part of Ronnie's reason, the fact that he desires to accomplish the further end in question would give that reason an implausibly self-regarding character even if it were true, as Schroeder maintains, that such a desire was a necessary condition of those ends being reason-providing. But Ronnie's reason in the case as Schroeder describes it *is* self-regarding. This suggests to me that the fact that Ronnie "likes to dance" plays a different role in that case than the general role that desire would play in the other cases I have mentioned if Schroeder's view were correct. What it suggests is that the psychological state that differentiates Ronnie's situation from Bradley's is not a desire (playing the same role as desires in these other cases), but rather the fact that Ronnie enjoys dancing, and that this fact is part of Ronnie's (unobjectionably self-regarding) reason, not just a background condition, as desires may be in these other cases. It is, of course, a further question, and a matter in dispute, whether the fact that he enjoys dancing provides Ronnie with a reason to go to the party only given the background condition that he desires pleasant experiences.

These issues arise again at the beginning of Schroeder's Chapter 8, where he briefly considers desires and "what people take pleasure in" as alternative candidates for the role of "the psychological state ... which most fundamentally explains the difference between Ronnie's and Bradley's reasons."[58] One way to decide between these alternatives would be to imagine cases in which Ronnie would take pleasure in dancing but does not know this and has no desire to dance, and to consider what reason he would have to go to the party if this were the case. Schroeder rejects this method of argument, on the ground that

---

58. *Slaves of the Passions*, p. 147.

our intuitions about such cases are unreliable. He says that we can't, for example, rule out the possibility that even if Ronnie has no desire to dance his reason for going to the party depends on some other desire, such as a desire to enjoy himself. It would be difficult, Schroeder says, to screen out the possibility of such a desire, or the possibility that Ronnie has some other desire that explains a reason for Ronnie to do what he enjoys. "So it seems more promising," he says, to proceed instead by "taking a closer look at what kind of psychological state is most *suited* to explain the existence of reasons" subject to constraints he has outlined earlier.[59]

We should note two things about this move. First, it is extremely plausible that Bradley, as well as Ronnie, desires to do what he enjoys, or that he has some other desire that explains why he has reason to do such things. It is therefore very plausible to suppose that the difference between Bradley and Ronnie lies somewhere else, such as in facts about *what* they enjoy. Second, Schroeder's strategy seems to involve a shift away from looking for an explanation of the difference between Ronnie's and Bradley's reasons to looking instead for a kind of psychological state that is suited to explain the existence of reasons in general, and Ronnie's reasons in particular. But, as I have said before, the idea that it is a psychological state that we should be looking for was made plausible to begin with by the fact that we were looking for an explanation of the difference between Ronnie's and Bradley's reasons. Although it seems very plausible that this difference must lie in their psychological states, the idea that all reasons are explained by psychological states is a different, and much more controversial claim, not obviously supported by the example of Ronnie and Bradley.

Frank Jackson also objected strongly to the idea that there might be normative properties in addition to the purely naturalistic properties with which they are coextensive. It is possible that he would not consider these objections to apply to normative properties understood in the minimal way I have proposed. But I should consider whether the objections he raises apply to my proposal. In the terms we have discussed, what Jackson is opposed to is taking the property signified by R to be something other than the grand property that Gibbard identified as the property signified by this relation.

---

59. *Slaves of the Passions*, p. 147.

Jackson mentions three objections. The first is that "it is hard to see how we could ever be justified in interpreting a language user's use of, say, 'right' as picking out a property distinct from that which the relevant purely descriptive predicates pick out, for we know that the complete story about how and when the language user produces the word 'right' can be given descriptively."[60] Suppose we know the set of quadruples $<p, x, c, a>$ such that a language user assents to "p is a reason for x, to do a in c." Does this amount to "the complete story" about how that language user understands the relation R? It seems to me that it does not. What we need to know further is how that language user responds when he believes that the relation $R(p, x, c, a)$ holds. In order to know whether the language user assents to $R(p, x, c, a)$ just when he or she takes it to be a "true thought" that p counts in favor of a for someone in c, we need to know whether he or she generally treats $R(p, x, c, a)$ as relevant to the question of whether to do a when he or she takes him or herself to be in circumstances c and believes p.

This also provides a basis for responding to Jackson's second objection, which is that "it is hard to see how the further properties could be of any ethical significance. Are we supposed to take seriously someone who says, 'I see that this action will kill many and save no one, but that is not enough to justify my not doing it; what really matters is that the action has an extra property such that only ethical terms are suited to pick out'? In short, the extra properties would be ethical idlers."[61] The property minimally signified by R, on my view, is not a "normative idler." To claim that $R(p, x, c, a)$ holds is precisely to claim that (for x in c) p justifies doing a; it is not to claim that p has some further property which does the justifying.

Finally, Jackson asks how we determine in which cases there is, in addition to some purely descriptive property, a normative property coextensive with it. The answer is that this is in each case a normative question: it depends on whether a particular p actually is a reason for someone in c to do a.

I have been defending the idea that there are irreducibly normative truths about reasons. But, as I have explained, I am not claiming that there is a relational property "in the natural world," that is to say, a naturalistic relational property, corresponding to the relational concept

60. Jackson, *From Metaphysics to Ethics*, p. 127.
61. Jackson, *From Metaphysics to Ethics*, p. 127.

"being a reason for." Normative truths, in my view, constitute a distinct realm and need no natural or special metaphysical reality in order to have the significance that we commonly grant them.

Given the limited nature of my claims of truth for normative assertions, it may be asked how much my view really differs from Gibbard's expressivism or Blackburn's quasi-realism. Both Gibbard and Blackburn allow for, or even embrace, the idea of normative claims being true in what they see as a minimal sense. And like them, I am claiming that normative judgments are about our reactions to the natural world, rather than about that world itself (specifically, in my case, about the *appropriateness* of these reactions). So it may seem that little difference remains. As a challenge to my view, this would be the correlate to challenges that have been made to Blackburn, that his quasi-realism was no different from realism.[62]

Despite these appearances, important differences remain. They have to do with the way in which the practical significance of normative commitments is explained, with the way in which interpersonal advice and disagreement about normative questions is interpreted, and with the sense in which the correctness of our normative commitments is independent of those commitments themselves. I will discuss these matters in the next lecture.

---

62. See Gideon Rosen, "Blackburn's *Essays in Quasi-Realism*," and Jamie Dreier, "Meta-ethics and the Problem of Creeping Minimalism." Dreier suggests (p. 37) that the difference between realism and expressivism lies in the fact that the former, but not the latter, appeals to normative *properties* in order to explain certain phenomena. So perhaps he would place my view on the "expressivist" side of this distinction (as I would not).

Lecture 3

Motivation and the Appeal of Expressivism

1. Two lines of argument have been offered against the idea that judgments about reasons for action can be true or false, and in favor of expressivist accounts of normative judgment. The first argument, which I responded to in Lecture 2, is that the idea of intrinsically normative truths has unacceptable metaphysical implications, and is incompatible with a scientific, or "naturalistic" view of the world. The second argument, which I will consider in this lecture, is that an account that interprets judgments about reasons as beliefs is unable to explain the practical significance of such judgments, in particular their connection with action.

This is often put by saying that such an account will be unable to explain how normative judgments motivate people to act. But it is not clear exactly what kind of explanation is thought to be required. The term "motivate" has a dual character. When it is said that only desires can motivate, and that beliefs are "motivationally inert," the motivation in question may seem to be a kind of causal efficacy. But "motivate" also has a rational, or even normative aspect: desires are not only supposed to cause actions but also to "rationalize" them, as Donald Davidson famously said.[1] I take this to mean, at least, that a desire makes an action (believed to promote its satisfaction) understandable, or perhaps even makes it "rational."

If to rationalize an action is to make it understandable, and even rational, for the agent to so act, then it would seem that an agent's belief that she had a reason to perform an action, even if it is a *belief*, could rationalize her action just as well as a desire could. So the

1. "Actions, Reasons, and Causes," p. 4.

supposed unique motivational efficacy of desires, and corresponding deficiency of cognitivist accounts of reasons, may lie in the former, causal, idea of motivation.

Desires come to us unbidden, and we may feel that they impel us to action. But this does not mean that an explanation of action in terms of the agent's desires is a causal explanation in a way in which an explanation in terms of the agent's beliefs about reasons is not. Beliefs about reasons are also not subject to our will or choice, and can have a demanding quality. The deeper point, however, is that neither in the case of desires nor in that of beliefs about reasons is this experience of "impulse" a direct experience of a cause. This feeling is simply an element of our momentary experience. If such experiences are generally followed by action this is because of some underlying neural mechanism that is equally causal in the two cases and in neither case an object of experience.

Even if the belief that one has a reason to act in a certain way can rationalize that action—that is to say, make sense of it—more needs to be said about how, and in what sense, such a belief can *explain* action. On my view, this explanation relies on the idea of a rational agent. A rational agent is, first, one that is capable of thinking about the reasons for certain actions or attitudes, and for reaching conclusions about which of these are good reasons. Second, a being is a rational agent only if the judgments that it makes about reasons make a difference to the actions and attitudes that it proceeds to have. A perfectly rational agent would always have attitudes and perform the actions that are appropriate according to the judgments about reasons that he or she accepts. A rational agent will, for example, generally intend to do those actions that he or she judges him or herself to have conclusive reason to do, and believe a proposition if he or she takes him or herself to have good evidence for its truth.[2]

More exactly, if a rational agent believes that p is a conclusive reason to do a, she generally will do a, and do it *for this reason.* That is to say, she will guide her movements in the ways that she takes p to count in favor of, and when asked why she is doing this she will cite p as a reason. What she will cite will be, in the first instance, p, the fact she takes to count in favor of a, rather than the fact that p is a reason to a, or her

---

2. I will discuss these stronger normative relations, such as *sufficient reason* and *conclusive reason*, in Lecture 5.

belief that this is the case. Appeal to the fact that p is a reason to a may come later, if her reference to p as a reason is challenged. Similar things are true about the relation between beliefs and beliefs about reasons for these beliefs, and about other attitudes and beliefs about reasons for them. If a rational agent believes that p is good evidence for q, hence a reason to believe that q, he or she will believe that q and will cite p as his or her reason.

A perfectly rational agent would always respond in these ways to his or her judgments about reasons. None of us is perfectly rational, but it is appropriate to call us rational agents just in case we come sufficiently close to meeting these standards. When a rational agent does something that he or she judges him or herself to have reason to do, this judgment makes sense of the action in normative terms and explains it, because the action is what one would expect of a rational agent who accepted that judgment. Presumably there is also a causal explanation of this connection, and of the more general uniformities that I have referred to, in virtue of which a being is a rational agent. But this causal explanation is another story, for neuroscientists to fill in.

This familiar idea of rational agency explains the practical significance of beliefs about reasons. If a rational agent judges p to be a reason to do a under certain circumstances, then he or she will normally treat p as weighing in favor of a on appropriate occasions. If he or she judges that p is conclusive reason to do a, then he or she will normally so act when the occasion arises, and his or her belief that p is a reason to a will explain this. If the agent does not so act—if he or she refuses to consider p as a reason, or declines to do a even though realizing that he or she is in circumstances in which he or she judges p to be a compelling reason to a, then the person is being irrational.

It may be objected that what is missing in cases in which a person intentionally fails to do what he judges himself to have conclusive reason to do is *motivation* to do that thing. This may be taken to show that even in the case of a perfectly rational agent, judgments about reasons alone are not sufficient to explain actions. An additional element of motivation is required.

This objection rests on a mistake. It is true that when a person intentionally does not do what he believes himself to have conclusive reason to do he fails to be adequately motivated to do this. And it is also true that when a person does what he believes himself to have conclusive reason to do (for that reason) he is motivated to do this.

This is not to say that there is, in the latter case, some further element that does the motivating, but only that in this case his judgment leads to action via the processes that are normal for a rational agent, and the agent is moved to act by the consideration he judges to be conclusive. In cases of irrationality these normal processes fail to work properly, and the agent is not "motivated" by this consideration.[3]

The conception of a rational agent that I am describing is both commonsensical and, in the present context, controversial. It is commonsensical because we all interpret ourselves and others as rational agents in this sense. It is controversial because it does a significant amount of work in my account, and may be thought to be philosophically question-begging, even if it seems obvious from an everyday point of view.

2. To see how this is so, compare my explanation of the connection between normative judgment and subsequent action with the explanations offered by expressivist theories. The early non-cognitivist R. M. Hare wrote that moral judgments must be understood as expressing the acceptance of imperatives because, he said, this is the only kind of judgment that is logically linked with action. That is, the only kind of judgment such that if a subsequent action of an appropriate kind is not performed it follows that the agent spoke insincerely, or did not understand what he or she was saying.[4] More recently, Allan Gibbard, in *Thinking How to Live*, analyzes judgments about reasons (not necessarily moral judgments but judgments about what one has most reason to do) as decisions about what to do, or the adoption of plans.[5] His idea, I take it, is not just that the states consisting of the adoption of plans *cause* subsequent actions that carry out these plans but that the adoption of a plan makes these subsequent actions rational, and perhaps makes it irrational to fail to undertake them. In his earlier book, *Wise Choices, Apt Feelings*, Gibbard interpreted normative judgments as expressing acceptance of norms, which then govern the agent's subsequent attitudes and actions insofar as he or she is not irrational.[6]

---

3. I am grateful to John Broome and Ralph Wedgwood for prompting me to respond to this objection.
4. *The Language of Morals*, pp. 20, 171–2.
5. *Thinking How to Live*, Chapter 3 *et passim*.
6. *Wise Choices, Apt Feelings*, Chapter 4.

Each of these accounts is like mine in seeking to explain the connection between more reflective states, involving an element of judgment or commitment, with subsequent responses of various kinds, including actions. And all of these accounts explain this connection by appealing to an ideal of rational agency: an agent will, insofar as he or she is not irrational, act in accord with imperatives or norms he or she accepts, carry out plans he or she has adopted, and, in my version, adopt attitudes in conformity with his or her assessments of the reasons for them.[7]

My account differs from the others, first, in the nature of the reflective state with which it begins. In expressivist accounts, this state is some kind of resolution or practical commitment: an attitude of accepting an imperative or norm, adopting a plan, or, in other expressivist accounts, expressing approval or some other "pro-attitude." The conception of rationality appealed to is just a matter of practical consistency, of "following through" on these attitudes. On my view, by contrast, the reflective state is one of judging something to be true, of having a certain belief. The practical import of this state lies in its distinctive content as a judgment or belief about reasons. There is therefore more work for the ideal of rationality to do, building a link between beliefs with this distinctive content and subsequent attitudes and action. It is still a matter of practical consistency, of "following through" on one's attitudes, but the connection may seem more controversial. It is not, as I have said, controversial in common-sense terms. Such a link is part of the idea of rationality that we normally employ. But many philosophers have held that this common-sense idea should not be accepted at face value, or is at least in need of explanation.

As Gibbard says, non-cognitivist accounts attempt to explain what it is to judge something to be a reason rather than taking this idea for granted, as I do.[8] These accounts start from the (psychological) idea of what it is for someone to treat something as a reason, rather than from the idea of what it is to *be* a reason. I also refer (in my characterization of a rational agent) to a psychological state of treating something as a reason, and what I say about this state is very similar to what Gibbard says. But I go beyond this, and attribute to rational agents beliefs about which things *are* reasons, and I describe them as responding to such beliefs.

Expressivist accounts avoid this. They provide an alternative account of the common-sense idea of treating something as a reason which, they believe, provides a deeper explanation of our normative thinking.

3. What must such an account do in order to be satisfactory? It should offer an interpretation of taking something to be a reason that fits with and explains the various kinds of practical significance that such states have. This is what Gibbard calls the question of *internal adequacy*: whether the expressivist analysis "accounts for everything internal to normative thinking, or everything internal that is intelligible."[9]

Expressivist theories were developed largely to explain the significance of normative judgments for the agent who makes them—to explain how such judgments "motivate" an agent. I will return to the question of the adequacy of expressivist explanations of this phenomenon. But I want first to consider their adequacy as explanations of the significance of normative judgment in interpersonal discourse, when we are giving advice, or discussing the justifiability of an action.

According to Gibbard, to judge that p is a reason to do a in circumstances c is to plan to weigh the fact that p in favor of doing a in such circumstances. It would seem to follow that to advise someone that p is a reason to a in her circumstances is to express my acceptance of a plan to weigh the fact that p in favor of a under such conditions. This does not seem to capture the normative grip that advice is intended to have on someone who believes what the adviser says. Why should she care what I plan to do? We might try to close this gap by ascending to a higher level: my advice could consist in expressing my acceptance of a plan to adopt the plan of weighing the fact that p in favor of a in her circumstances. But the gap remains. Why should she care what plans I plan to adopt? My advice seems to get a grip on the recipient only if she plans, to at least some degree, to conform her normative thinking to mine.[10]

---

9. *Thinking How to Live*, p. 186. Gibbard contrasts the question of "internal" adequacy with external "commentary on normative thinking, concepts and their truth-makers that aren't part of normative thinking itself, or equivalent to it." This contrast is not totally clear, but I take it that he would count the question of whether normative judgments correspond to facts "in the world" as an external question, whereas the question of whether a normative judgment would be correct even if I did not accept it is internal, because it is stated in purely normative terms.

10. Gibbard gives an account of possible forms of normative discourse that proceeds very much along these lines in *Wise Choices, Apt Feelings*, pp. 174–83, arguing, essentially, that the authority of advice depends in most cases on the audience's acceptance of norms of convergence of the kind just mentioned.

I believe that the structure I have just described remains the same if we take advice to express the acceptance of norms rather than the adoption of plans. Interpreting advice as an imperative to weigh *p* in favor of doing *a* has the same difficulties, and adds a rather unpleasant air of ordering the person around. Taking my advice as expressing approval of weighing *p* in favor of *a* avoids this unpleasant air, and may sound more plausible. But this is in part because approval can mean so many different things. I can, for example, approve of someone's weighing *p* in favor of *a* because I find this flattering, or because it will lead the person to do something that will benefit me. In order to capture the idea of advice, the relevant kind of approval needs to be specified more exactly. "Expressing approval" appears to describe what is going on in giving advice if (I would say only if) we take it to be approval of the person's attitude *on the ground that* what he or she takes to be a reason is actually one.

Similar problems arise for expressivist interpretations of normative claims offered as justification. Suppose someone objects to my having done *a*, and I claim in response that *p* was good reason to do *a*. If this is just to express my plan to weigh the fact that *p* in favor of *a* in such circumstances, or my acceptance of a plan to plan to weigh the fact that *p* in favor of *a*, why should this carry any weight with the person who has complained? It is already obvious that I plan to behave in these ways. That is what the person is objecting to. Again, it seems to me that the same problem holds for interpretations of normative judgments as expression of acceptance of norms, as imperatives, or as expressions of approval.

The account I am defending avoids these difficulties. According to this account, when I offer someone advice, saying that *p* is a reason for him or her to do *a*, I am not expressing a plan or an imperative but, rather, calling that person's attention to what I claim to be a fact, independent of both of us, about what one has reason to do. As a fact independent of either of us it is something we can discuss and potentially disagree about, just as we can disagree about who was prime minister of Great Britain in 1917. If the person believes what I say, then this gets a grip on his subsequent behavior in virtue of his being rational. Whether he agrees or not, my claim has normative force for someone in his position *if it is correct*, its force lying in the fact, if it is a fact, that *p* actually is a reason for him to do *a*.[11]

---

11. As I argued in Lecture 1.

The same holds in the case of justification. If a person has objected to my doing *a*, we disagree about whether this action was justified. Whether the other person agrees with it or not, my claim that *p* was a reason for me to do *a* responds to his challenge, in a way that expressing my acceptance of a norm, or a plan, or an attitude of approval does not.

The situation is much the same with respect to another condition of internal adequacy that Gibbard mentions. This is that an adequate account of normative judgments must do justice to the thought that our judgments about reasons can be mistaken and, if they are correct, would be correct even if we did not make them. To take an example that Gibbard cites, an internally adequate account of normative judgments should be able to make sense of what a person is thinking when he thinks that it is wrong to kick dogs for fun and that this would be wrong even if he, misguidedly, believed that dog kicking was perfectly acceptable behavior.[12]

The thought that I might be mistaken in thinking that *p* is a reason for me to do *a* might be understood as expressing my plan to count the fact that *p* in favor of *a*, in circumstances like mine, but at the same time also expressing my acceptance of higher-order norms governing the acceptance of such plans and my recognition that, conceivably, these norms might turn out to support revision of my current attitude.[13] But it is also intelligible to think that these higher-order norms might themselves be mistaken. One way of expressing this would simply be through the thought that I might come, in the future, to hold different higher-order norms, ones that would mandate changing my attitudes toward *p* and *a*. But this would not capture the thought that those attitudes might be mistaken, since it does not distinguish between changes that are corrections and ones that involve falling into error.

An expressivist might try to make this distinction by appeal to yet higher-order norms that might require change in my current norms of attitude revision. Since it is intelligible to think that I might also be mistaken in accepting *these* norms, the possibility of regress looms again. As in the case of advice and justification, the problem flows from the fact that, on an expressivist account, the attitudes appealed

12. Gibbard, *Wise Choices, Apt Feelings*, pp. 174–83. Blackburn makes a similar point in "Errors and the Phenomenology of Value," p. 153.

13. Blackburn, *Ruling Passions*, p. 293; Gibbard, *Wise Choices, Apt Feelings*, Chapters 8 and 9, esp. pp. 168ff.

to, at any level, to mark the difference between changes in attitude that are corrections and those that are errors, must be attitudes that the person in question currently holds. This means that the possibility that one might be fundamentally in error in one's normative beliefs is not intelligible on this account. The account can make sense of the thought that someone else might be in fundamental normative error, however. So, as Andy Egan argues, the implication of this expressivist view seems to be that each of us must regard him or herself as uniquely immune to this possibility.[14] This is an odd result.

A cognitivist view of the kind I am advocating avoids these difficulties. It cuts off the regress at the start by holding that when one makes a normative judgment one is claiming that this judgment is correct, rather than merely expressing one's acceptance of some attitude that supports it. A cognitivist would agree that if one of one's normative judgments is mistaken then there is a (correct) norm of attitude revision which would, in the light of certain information that one now does not possess, call for the revision of this judgment. But the thought that one's judgment might be incorrect does not involve endorsement of any particular such higher-order attitude.[15]

4. It should come as no surprise that my view is, in these ways, more in accord with the common-sense understanding of normative judgments than expressivist interpretations are, since my account begins by taking the common-sense idea of a reason at face value. But perhaps this involves accepting more of our ordinary normative thinking than is "intelligible," as Gibbard puts it.[16] So I need to consider whether aspects of ordinary thinking that I accept should be rejected.

14. See Egan, "Quasi-Realism and Fundamental Moral Error." Egan's charge, in the last section of his paper, that Blackburn's view leads to a crude subjectivism, seems to me mistaken. I am concerned here with Egan's argument in earlier sections.
15. Even if the cognitivist can avoid this regress problem, however, I have some doubts about the intelligibility of the thought that all of one's normative judgments might be mistaken, even on a cognitivist view. Might I be mistaken in thinking that pain is in general to be avoided rather than to be sought? I do not see how I could be. What kind of mistake might I be making? To ask this question is to ask what there is about my current view that some norm would (correctly) find faulty. It is not to endorse any particular such norm, or higher-order norm of norm adoption. Still, the idea that there might be some such fault seems inconceivable. But this inconceivability is a substantive matter.
16. *Thinking How to Live*, p. 185.

The state of taking something to be a reason, as I interpret it, is a purely psychological state, just as "naturalistic" as the state of adopting a plan, accepting a norm, or feeling approval. Even a belief in witches is a naturalistic psychological state in this sense. One possible worry is that, like beliefs in witches, beliefs in facts about reasons are *about* something non-naturalistic, and are suspect for that reason.

The objection might be that the idea that there are non-natural truths is metaphysically odd. I have explained in my previous lecture why I believe this is not so. Normative truths do not require strange metaphysical truth-makers. Such truths are determined by the standards of the normative domain itself. Even if this is accepted, however, it might be claimed that these standards are insufficiently well defined to determine what is true, normatively speaking.[17] I believe that this is a serious worry, and I will address it in Lecture 4.

Simon Blackburn raises two further objections to a cognitivist interpretation of normative thinking, objections that I believe are shared by many non-cognitivists. He writes that this way of understanding ethical judgments is "destabilized" by "questions of epistemology and of why we should be concerned about the ethical properties of things."[18] I will take up the question of epistemology in my next lecture. But there are several things to be said here about Blackburn's second question.

First, it makes a difference that Blackburn is speaking here about *ethical* truths and beliefs, rather than, more generally, about truths and beliefs about reasons. There is an intelligible question of why we should care about the moral rightness of our actions. But this is a *normative* question, one that asks for a reason and is answered by giving one. As I pointed out in my first lecture, things are quite different when the subject is normative truths in general. There may still be an epistemological question about how we come to know such truths, but the question "Why should one care about what reasons one has?" is nonsensical if it is understood to be asking for a reason.

Perhaps Blackburn's question "why should we care?," asked about normative truth in general, is not one that asks for a reason, but is rather a question about the rational authority of reasons, a version of Korsgaard's question of how normative truths could "get a grip on" an

17. A failure of what Crispin Wright calls "cognitive command." See *Truth and Objectivity*, pp. 88ff.
18. *Ruling Passions*, p. 80.

agent. If so, this would support the suggestion that I made in my first lecture, that not only Kantians but also proponents of many other theories, including some desire theories and, in this case, expressivist views, believe that the authority of reasons must be grounded in something that an agent already accepts. According to Korsgaard, it must be grounded "in the agent's own will," and this would also be the view of some expressivists, on the interpretation I am considering, if accepting a plan or imperative is an expression of the agent's will.

This brings us to the question of the "internal adequacy" of an expressivist account of the significance of normative judgments for the person who makes them. Since the question of whether something is a reason is a question one asks in deciding what one's "will" in the matter is to be—what plan one is to have, or what norms one is going to accept—grounding the answer to such questions in the agent's will, or plan, etc. is not a possibility for the agent him or herself. I may plan to weigh *p* in favor of doing *a* in certain circumstances, but the normative force of that plan *for me* depends on my assumption that I have good reason to have it, and the same is true for any higher-order plan, or norm. Kant believed that he had resources to stop this potential regress because he thought there were normative attitudes that were required simply by being a rational agent. I do not find his arguments for this convincing. But in any event this way out is not available to an expressivist.

From an agent's own point of view, conclusions about what he or she has reason to do must be grounded ultimately in other conclusions about reasons. It may seem that this account is also threatened by a regress.[19] One can always ask, of any conclusion about reasons, whether that conclusion is in fact correct—whether, and why, the fact that it claims to be a reason really is such a reason. But this is just an instance of the general truth that every argument has to begin somewhere. The regress that threatens an expressivist account, or any will-based theory of reasons, is different. Any plan (or acceptance of a norm, or attitude of approval) needs to be backed up by a judgment of another sort, one about reasons. The question is not "Do I plan to..." (or "Do I approve of...") but "*Should* I plan to...? Do I have good reason to do this?" Answering this question in the affirmative brings the process to a close, unless I have good reason to doubt this conclusion.

19. As Christine Korsgaard charges. See *The Sources of Normativity*, p. 33.

As I said earlier, expressivism was originally developed as a way of explaining the problem of motivation or, as I would put it, the rational connection between normative judgment and action. It does indeed explain this connection. If I plan to do something (or accept an imperative to do it, etc.) then I am irrational if, without rejecting this plan, I consciously disregard it in deciding what to do. But a conclusion about what an agent must do (or must see as a reason) insofar as he or she is not irrational is not the same thing as a conclusion about what the agent has reason to do. A conclusion of the latter kind depends not only on the agent's own states of mind (plans or other attitudes), but also on the reasons that support them. And this is true even from the agent's own point of view. So an explanation of the rational connection between normative judgment and action is not a full account of the normative force of those judgments even from the agent's own point of view.

5. A less extreme way of understanding Blackburn's question is to take it as a challenge to the cognitivist's ability to explain the rational connection between normative judgment and action—the question of how a (mere) belief about reasons could explain action. This is a genuine question, and I have offered an answer to it earlier in this lecture. It does follow from that answer, however, that if the acceptance of a normative judgment is a form of belief, it differs from other beliefs—such as empirical beliefs and mathematical beliefs—in being rationally related to intentions and actions, rather than merely to other beliefs. By a rational relation I mean a connection that it is irrational to deny. Factual beliefs can have a weaker form of "rational connection with action" insofar as they are beliefs about things that *are* reasons, such as a belief that a piece of metal is sharp, or that a certain substance is poison. A person who has such a belief can be open to rational criticism for not treating the fact that he or she believes as a reason. But the failure to do so is not always irrational; it may just be mistaken. By contrast, it is irrational to judge some consideration to be a reason to do some action, and then refuse to treat it as a reason.

It might be maintained that if acceptance of a normative judgment has this kind of rational connection with action, then it is not a belief, since (by definition?) beliefs do not have such connections. Absent some further argument, however, this claim seems to me merely stipulative. Little turns on the term "belief" as long as it is recognized that judgments about reasons can be correct or incorrect independent of their being made, and thus that they behave like beliefs in interpersonal argument and disagreement.

Arguments have, however, been offered against the possibility of a state (whether it is called a belief or not) that has the features I am claiming for the acceptance of a normative judgment. "Direction of fit" arguments maintain that no state can both have standards of correctness (a "mind-to-world" direction of fit) and rational connections to intention and action (a "world-to-mind direction of fit").[20] This claim has some plausibility as long as "the world" in question is taken to be the natural world of physical objects, causes and effects. For any proposition p about that world, a belief that p has a mind-to-world direction of fit—that is to say, a person is open to rational criticism if he or she does not modify this belief in the face of credible evidence that p is false. Any such p might also be a good reason for some action a. If so, then a person who believes that p and fails to treat it as a reason for a is making a normative error and thus open to a kind of rational criticism. But this criticism is appropriate in virtue of the truth of a further normative claim that p is a reason to do a in circumstances c, not simply in virtue of the fact that the agent believes that p. So a belief that p is linked to standards of correctness (must "fit the world") simply by being the kind of state that it is, but it is not rationally tied to action in this same way.

This argument depends, however, on the assumption that the belief in question is a belief about the natural world. If it is not—if the relevant standard of correctness is not "fitting with" the natural world but some other form of correctness—then the second half of the argument fails. In particular, if the belief in question is a belief that p is, in the agent's circumstances, a good reason to do a, then it is true simply in virtue of being the kind of state that it is (and not in virtue of any further normative fact) that a person who has that belief would be irrational in refusing to treat p as such a reason. The plausibility of the argument that a state cannot have both "mind-to-world" and "world-to-mind" directions of fit is limited to cases in which "the world" referred to in both cases is the natural world. The tendency to think that this argument rules out interpreting normative judgments as a kind of belief is thus another instance of the tendency mentioned in

---

20. See, for example, Michael Smith, *The Moral Problem*, pp. 112–25.

my second lecture, to identify the set of all things independent of us about which our opinions can be correct or incorrect with "the natural world."

6. Nonetheless, there are reasonable questions about how the idea of correctness that is supposed to apply to normative judgments is to be understood. On expressivist views the essential content of such judgments is given by some "active" element, such as adopting a plan or accepting an imperative, which renders these judgments incapable of being true or false. My strategy has been to "export" this active element—to account for the distinctive practical significance of judgments about reasons by appeal to the idea of rational agency. The remaining content—the claim that something is a reason—is left as something that can be true or false, that one can be mistaken about, and that can function in interpersonal discourse like any other proposition. The question is how this residual content—the claim of correctness—is to be understood. The obvious significance of judgments about reasons lies in their rational links with action. But if this is all there is, then it would seem that the "cognitivism" I am proposing will just be another form of expressivism.

This question might be answered by a metaphysical account of the truth conditions of normative judgments. But the interpretation of normative truth that I defended in Lecture 2 rules out such an account. The idea that normative judgments are correct when they correspond to the normative facts is no explanation if these "facts" are, as I have suggested, merely "the reflection of true thoughts." So, it may be said, the question remains what the content of these thoughts is and what makes these thoughts true.

At this point, I believe, defenders of irreducibly normative truths must dig in their heels. The idea of some consideration's being a good reason for some action or attitude is a perfectly intelligible one. To believe that some consideration is a reason is not the same thing as treating that consideration as a reason in subsequent deliberation— there is such a thing as irrationally failing to act in accord with the reasons one believes oneself to have. Given the intelligibility of this idea, and the fact that taking it at face value provides the best fit with our practices of thinking about reasons and arguing about them with others, we should reject it only if it gives rise to some difficulties that cannot be answered satisfactorily. I have argued that the idea of irreducibly normative truths does not have implausible metaphysical implications, and that the connection between beliefs about reasons and subsequent action can be satisfactorily explained.

Aside from worries about how the idea of the correctness of normative judgments is to be understood, however, questions may also be raised about the importance that this idea should have for us. I have suggested that it is important in two contexts: in making sense of the idea that the correctness or incorrectness of our normative judgments is independent of our making those judgments, and in interpreting interpersonal discourse and disagreement about normative questions. Each of these forms of importance may be questioned.

Suppose that you and I disagree about whether the fact that someone injured me is good reason for me to injure him in return. Perhaps I maintain that it is, and you deny this. Suppose we go on arguing about this for some time. We each adduce all the considerations that either of us can think of to get the other to change his mind, but we still disagree. It would be pointless and empty for me, at this point, to insist, as if it were a trump card, "But my view is *correct*. The fact that he injured me *is* a reason!" Such an appeal to "correctness" would be mere foot-stomping.[21]

Similarly, in the intrapersonal case, if one believes that something is a reason, it is natural to think that it would be a reason whether or not one believed that it was. But why should this be so important to us? If we are convinced that something is a reason, and are ready to act on it, why should we be concerned to have the imprimatur of some independent standard of correctness? As Nietzsche would say, the need for the prop of such a standard betrays a kind of weakness.[22] In a similar vein, Simon Blackburn says that it is sad that some people should feel this need for Apollonian authority, rather than being content to accept the motivation provided by their own, contingent, emotions and desires.[23]

As I will say in my next lecture, I think there are cases in which the interpersonal version of this worry points toward a genuine issue. But neither worry provides grounds for rejecting concern with the idea that normative judgments can be correct or incorrect. At the conclusion of

---

21. As Christine Korsgaard observes. See *The Sources of Normativity*, p. 38.
22. See *On the Genealogy of Morality*, Third Essay, esp. sections 26–8.
23. *Ruling Passions*, pp. 88–91.

an unsuccessful attempt to persuade someone, it would indeed be unhelpful foot-stomping to insist, as if it were a further point in your favor, "But my view is correct!" (Of course you think it is correct.) This is equally true when the disagreement is about some matter of empirical fact. So it does not show that the idea of correctness is misplaced, and better done away with, in the case of normative disagreement.

Moreover, the idea that when we disagree about a normative question there is some fact of the matter we are disagreeing about, independent of each of us, which neither has any special authority to determine, provides if anything a more attractive picture of the relation between us than the idea that we are each simply trying to get the other to adopt the plan that we have adopted. Of course, the fact that this interpretation of disagreement is attractive, if it is, is not any reason to think that it is true. My aim in mentioning the attractiveness of the idea is just to rebut the suggestion that to be concerned that there be such a notion of correctness betrays a desire to claim an implausible and unattractive kind of authority for one's position.

Similarly, in the intrapersonal case, when several alternative courses of action seem appealing it does not indicate a kind of weakness to ask oneself which course one really has more reason to follow. The idea that this does reflect a kind of weakness may derive from thinking that being concerned with the correctness of one's normative beliefs involves looking for some authority "outside of ourselves" that will tell us what we ought to do. But this idea of an "authority" is a misleading metaphor. For any standard, in the form of a set of principles or precepts, there is the question, "Why do that?" But when I arrive at a conclusion about the correctness of a normative judgment—such as that I really do have reason to do what will save my life, or to avoid pain—there is no such further question. These conclusions carry their own normative authority, as it were. They do not need to derive it from some further source. The question of correctness is the question of whether they do have this authority—whether the considerations in question are really reasons. There is no further question beyond this one. There are, however, questions about how we can know that this is the case. I will turn to these in my next lecture.

Lecture 4
Epistemology and Determinateness

1. I have claimed that there are irreducibly normative truths about reasons, and that the essential normative element in such truths is a relation $R(p, x, c, a)$ that holds between a fact, an agent in certain circumstances, and an action or attitude. The idea that there are truths about when this relation holds, does not, I argued, have troubling metaphysical implications. To claim that something is a reason is just to claim that it bears this relation to some agent and action: nothing more. No metaphysically weightier property is required in order for truths about reasons to have the significance we attach to them. Nor, I have argued, is it puzzling why (most) normative facts supervene on facts about the natural world.

But if truths about reasons represent a *sui generis* class of facts, distinct from natural facts, it may seem puzzling how we could come to know such facts. John Mackie, for example, claims that if we were aware of these facts "it would have to be by some special faculty of moral perception or intuition, utterly different from our ordinary ways of knowing everything else." He continues:

When we ask the awkward question, how we can be aware of this authoritative prescriptivity, of the truth of these distinctively ethical premises or of the cogency of this distinctively ethical pattern of reasoning, none of our ordinary accounts of sensory perception or introspection or the framing and confirming of explanatory hypotheses or inference or logical construction or conceptual analysis, or any combination of these, will provide a satisfactory answer; 'a special sort of intuition' is a lame answer, but it is the one to which the clear headed objectivist is compelled to resort.[1]

1. *Ethics: Inventing Right and Wrong*, pp. 38–9. Similarly, Paul Benacerraf writes that a typical account of the truth conditions of number theory or set theory will depict them as conditions on objects "whose nature, as normally conceived, places them beyond the reach of the better understood means of human cognition (e.g. sense perception and the like)" ("Mathematical Truth," p. 409).

Mackie is here talking about objective *ethical* truths, but as I said in Lecture 2, I believe he would say the same about normative truths in general. A satisfactory response to this objection will have two components, one negative, one positive. The negative component consists in arguing against the idea that normative facts would be a special kind of entity, which we could "get in touch with" only through a faculty analogous to sensory perception. The positive component would be an account of the kind of thinking through which we can come to know normative truths.

What gives rise to distinctive epistemological questions about empirical knowledge, and makes a causal theory of knowledge seem like an appropriate answer to these questions, is the fact that it is part of the content of most empirical judgments that they are about objects that are distant from us in space. If information is to get from them to us, how is this to happen except by their having a causal impact on our sensory surfaces? Transfer of information by a non-causal process—some form of "intuition"—would be a strange and implausible alternative.

But things are quite different in the case of normative facts and mathematical facts. Nothing in the content of normative or mathematical judgments suggests that they are about objects with any particular spatio-temporal location at all, hence in particular not one "outside of us." But if these facts have no spatio-temporal location, this may be taken as ground for thinking that there is, after all, a special problem about how we could come to know them. For if these facts are "outside of space and time" the problem of explaining how information could get from them to us seems even greater than in the case of empirical truths. No causal link can bridge the gap, so some mysterious form of intuition seems to be required. But here the spatial metaphor has simply gotten out of hand. The idea of a region of existence "outside of space and time," and hence more inaccessible to us, is one we should not accept. If we reject this metaphor, however, we are still left with the question of how we discover truths about such matters.

It seems that we can discover normative truths and mathematical truths simply by thinking about these subjects in the right way. To provide the positive component of a satisfactory response to Mackie's objection we need to describe these "ways of thinking" in a way that makes plausible the claim that they are ways of arriving at knowledge about the subject matters in question.

In order to do this, it would be helpful first to provide a general characterization of these domains in their own terms (i.e. in normative, or mathematical terms). Such an overall account of the subject can help us to see what thinking about that subject involves, and thereby to see why more specific principles are valid. Ideally, it could also respond to a problem mentioned in Lectures 2 and 3 by providing assurance that all or at least many statements about the subject in question have determinate truth values, whether we can discover them or not, and that these truth values are "independent of us." As will be clear from the examples I will go on to discuss, overall accounts of a subject can vary greatly in the degree to which they achieve these aims, in particular in the degree of support they provide to the idea that statements about that subject matter have determinate truth values.

The urge to do justice to the idea that normative statements, or mathematical statements, have determinate truth values independent of us is one thing that draws people toward metaphysically "thicker" ideas of normative or mathematical facts. This fuels epistemological worries about how we could be in touch with such facts, in reaction to which it becomes appealing to interpret these facts as dependent on us—creations of our thinking or our will—and therefore accessible by us.

In order to avoid this cycle, what is needed is an overall account of the subject matter of a domain that fits with a plausible epistemology in the right way. That is, an account that makes clear how we can arrive at knowledge of that subject by thinking about it in the right way while also allowing for the possibility that some facts about the subject may outrun our ability to discover them, thereby avoiding an implausible verificationism.

A natural objection to this strategy for dealing with the tension between epistemology and realism is that it just pushes the epistemological problem back one step. An overall account of the kind I have been imagining of the normative or mathematical domain will itself be a very general normative or mathematical claim. So there remains the question of how we can know *this* claim to be true. The response I will offer is that (given the adequacy of what I called above the negative component of a response to Mackie's challenge) the method of reflective equilibrium provides a satisfactory answer to this problem.

The problems I have been discussing at a very abstract level arise in very similar ways with regard to both mathematical facts and normative facts, despite the important differences between these domains. In the next section I will discuss in more detail how they arise for set theory, which seems to me to present a particularly clear example. In section 3, I will discuss the method of reflective equilibrium, and defend the claim that it is the appropriate response to the problem just mentioned. Turning then in section 4 to the problems of normative truths and knowledge of them, I will argue that the general conclusions reached in the case of set theory carry over to the normative domain, but that the prospects for finding a satisfactory overall account of that domain are much more limited.

2. There is not a *greater* epistemological problem about mathematical judgments than about empirical ones, but a problem or problems of a different kind. The problem is not how we could "be in touch with" the abstract structures that mathematics is about, but how we can characterize these structures in a way that makes clear which principles and modes of reasoning about them are valid, and that supports the idea that questions about them have determinate truth values.

The subject matter of arithmetic, for example, is adequately characterized by saying that it includes zero and all and only those other numbers reached from zero by repeated applications of the successor function. This characterization seems evidently true and non-arbitrary. Since the truth values of arithmetical statements are determined, ultimately, by facts about the successor relation, this characterization supports the idea that arithmetical statements have determinate truth value (unless this description of an infinite domain is seen as unintelligible). We are capable of thinking about and comparing particular finite strings in this sequence, $0, S0, SS0, \ldots$ It is therefore not mysterious how we can arrive at basic truths of arithmetic "just by thinking about them." Moreover, on the basis of this characterization of the domain, we can recognize as true general axioms (such as the Peano postulates), which can then be used to establish particular theorems about numbers. Gödel's results show that any consistent formal system will leave some sentences of the system undecided, but this does not mean that the sentences that are undecidable in some particular system have no determinate truth value.

In the case of set theory we have a set of axioms that are very generally accepted. But these axioms would seem like arbitrary stipulations if we did not have some way of thinking about sets, independent of these axioms, in the light of which they seem obviously correct.

What kind of thinking is this? What are we doing when we are thinking about sets if this thinking is not a mysterious kind of perception? In a few cases this seems to be a matter of seeing what is "included in the concept of a set." For example, a set is understood as a collection of objects, and has no properties other than having these members. So the axiom of extensionality, which says that no two distinct sets can have exactly the same members, seems to follow from our understanding of what a set is. Most axioms are not of this character, however, even ones that seem entirely unproblematic. For example, the axiom of pairing says that if a and b are sets, then there is a set c whose members are just a and b. This may not be a conceptual truth—something that is "included in the very concept of a set." But it seems obviously true—something that anyone who understands the concept of set could hardly deny—because the way in which c is defined in terms of, or constructed out of, a and b is so clear and apparently unproblematic.

Consider a more complex example, the so-called axiom schema of replacement. Say that an open sentence "$M(x, y)$" defines a function on a set z if for every x in z there is a unique set y such that "$M(x, y)$" is true. An instance of the axiom schema of replacement then says that for any set z, there is a set w that contains just those things that bear M to some member of z. (This is the set obtained by "replacing" each element of z with the set assigned to it by the function defined by M.) This way of defining, or constructing, new sets from given sets is not as simple as in the case of the pair set axiom, and its consequences are less obvious. But the axiom schema of replacement is widely accepted both because of its intrinsic plausibility and because it leads to very plausible theorems, without, as far as anyone can tell after decades of use, generating any implausible conclusions, let alone contradictions.[2]

I take these to be good examples of how we come to have knowledge of sets. They seem to me to serve as a useful corrective to the tendency to think that such knowledge must come from one of two sources: either by derivation from the concept of a set, or via some form of intuition of the realm of sets, analogous to perception. The former seems to limit set theory to conceptual truths; and the latter seems mysterious. This might be called "the conceptual/intuitive dilemma." It seems to me untenable, not because there is no distinction

2. For discussion, see Boolos, "The Iterative Conception of Set," p. 500; Parsons, *Mathematical Thought and its Objects*, pp. 134, 339.

between the two alternatives it describes, but because it describes each of these alternatives in a misleading way.

As to the "conceptual" horn of the dilemma, the modes of thinking that support set-theoretic axioms do not consist simply in recognizing conceptual truths.[3] This is shown by the reasoning leading to the pair set axiom, and the axiom schema of replacement. But this reasoning does not rely on a puzzling form of intuition, as the second horn of the dilemma suggests. It may involve a kind of "mental picturing," but this picturing is not plausibly understood as a form of "intuitive contact" with the realm of sets. It is rather a matter of representing to ourselves how one set can be characterized in terms of others, in a way that is so clear as to leave us with no doubt that there is such a set.

Not every form of reasoning in support of set-theoretic axioms has this form. I already mentioned that the axiom schema of replacement derives support not only from intuitive plausibility of the kind I have just described but also from its fruitfulness: from the plausibility of its consequences (and the fact that it has not led to implausible ones). Axioms can be supported simply by reasoning of the later kind. As Gödel famously observed:

There might exist axioms so abundant in their verifiable consequences, shedding so much light on a whole field, and yielding such powerful methods for solving problems…that, no matter whether they are intrinsically necessary, they would have to be accepted at least in the same sense as an well-established physical theory.[4]

This form of reasoning for arriving at conclusions about sets relies on the plausibility of some particular judgments about sets, which seem clearly correct even after careful reflection. Additional claims are then justified on the basis of their ability to explain and unify these judgments. Arguing in this way for more and more axioms, we might build up a more and more complete account of the set-theoretic domain.

This process is still piecemeal. What is lacking, and would be desirable if we could attain it, is an overall account of the domain of sets, analogous to our conception of the natural numbers. An overall account of this kind would do several things. First, it could characterize the domain in a way that would support the idea that questions

3. Nor are these modes of thinking "combinatorial" in the sense Benacerraf uses, i.e. matters of calculation or derivation from axioms. See "Mathematical Truth," p. 407.
4. "What Is Cantor's Continuum Problem?," p. 477.

about this domain have definite truth values, whether or not it is possible for us to determine what these are. Second, it could provide a rationale for more specific axioms, perhaps including axioms that would settle important outstanding questions. I will describe two candidates for such an overall account, which provide helpful examples for our later discussion of the normative domain.

The first of these is what is sometimes called Naïve Set theory, according to which every predicate F determines a set consisting of those things *a* such that F*a*. This idea had greater currency among philosophers than among mathematicians. (Quine, for example, regarded it as particularly important.[5]) It is well known to lead to contradictions, such as Russell's Paradox, involving the set of all sets that are not members of themselves. The failure of this conception of sets led Quine to conclude that set theory was condemned to being defined only by piecemeal collections of axioms, which seem arbitrary in the absence of some overall account of the subject they describe. There are, however, other more plausible ways of understanding the domain of sets.

One such characterization is provided by what has been called the Iterative Conception of Set.[6] According to this conception, the universe of sets consists of just those that would be formed in the following process: Begin, at stage 0, with the empty set or a list of specified elements. At stage $n+1$ form all sets of the basic elements and the sets that were created at previous stages. For each limit ordinal λ, at stage λ form the set of all sets formed at stage α for all $\alpha<\lambda$. The Iterative Conception provides a rationale for most of the standard axioms of accepted set theory. As I have stated it, the account is vague or incomplete in a number of ways. First, it appeals at various points to the idea of "all sets" "formed" at previous stages, and these ideas seem to need further specification.[7] Second, it remains unspecified how far the construction extends. It may be said to extend though "all" of the transfinite ordinals, but how far is that? The ordinals themselves are sets, hence part of what is to be specified.

Leaving these questions aside, we can see that the Naïve Conception and the Iterative Conception take off from two different ideas of

5. See the discussion in Parsons, *Mathematics and Philosophy*, pp. 197–205.

6. On this conception and the adequacy of the basis it provides for axioms of set theory, see Shoenfield, "Axioms of Set Theory," Boolos, "The Iterative Conception of Set," Parsons, "What Is the Iterative Conception of Set?," and Boolos, "Iteration Again."

7. As Parsons notes in "What Is the Iterative Conception of Set?" there are also questions about how the idea of "earlier and later" in the sequence is to be understood.

what is crucial to a set. The Naïve Conception focuses on the idea of sets as *extensions* of predicates. On this view sets depend on the predicates that define them. The Iterative Conception on the other hand expresses the idea of sets as *collections*.[8] On this view sets depend on (are "formed out of") their members. No mention is made of predicates in this process of formation, but it is presupposed that the members of a set exist independently of that set. This rules out the possibility of a set being a member of itself. The Naïve Conception had to be rejected since it led to contradiction, but one might say in retrospect that it could already have been objected to on this ground.[9]

The Iterative Conception of set provides an intuitive rationale for the axioms of Zermelo-Frankel set theory.[10] But these axioms leave open some important questions about sets, such as the truth of the Continuum Hypothesis—the hypothesis that there are no transfinite sets that are larger than the set of all natural numbers but smaller than the set of all sets of natural numbers. To resolve this question, and others, we need to find additional axioms. These additional axioms, and any general characterization of the domain of sets, would be justified mainly in the way that Gödel described: by their ability to explain and unify more specific conclusions about sets that seem to be true. (Ideally, they would also be supported by an augmented version of the Iterative Conception, or some other overall description of the realm of sets.) It might be said, then, that the axioms of set theory are justified ultimately by what Rawls called the method of reflective equilibrium.[11] It is worth pausing to consider to what degree this is so, and what kind of justification this method can provide.

3. In broad outline, the method of reflective equilibrium can be described as follows.[12] One begins by identifying a set of considered

---

8. On this contrast, see Parsons, *Mathematical Thought and its Objects*, pp. 113–22.

9. Although a theory of "non-well-founded" sets, which allows for this possibility, has also been explored.

10. See the papers by Shoenfield and Boolos cited in note 6.

11. As suggested in Parsons, *Mathematical Thought and Its Objects*, pp. 324–5.

12. The method was given its name by Rawls, who first proposed it in 1951 in "An Outline of a Decision Procedure for Ethics," later (in *A Theory of Justice*, p. 20, footnote 7) noting "parallel remarks concerning the justification of the principles of deductive and inductive inference" in Nelson Goodman's *Fact, Fiction, and Forecast*. Rawls modified and developed the method in *A Theory of Justice*, section 9, and in "The Independence of Moral Theory." The discussion that follows draws on my "Rawls on Justification."

judgments, of any level of generality, about the subject in question.[13] These are judgments that seem clearly to be correct and seem so under conditions that are conducive to making good judgments of the relevant kind about this subject matter. If the subject in question is morality, for example, they may be judgments about the rightness or wrongness of particular actions, general moral principles, or judgments about the kind of considerations that are relevant to determining the rightness of actions. In the case of set theory, considered judgments might include general principles of set existence or judgments about the existence of particular sets. The method does not privilege judgments of any particular type—those about particular cases, for example—as having special justificatory standing.

The next step in the method is to formulate general principles that would "account for" these judgments. By this Rawls means principles such that, had one simply been trying to apply them, rather than trying directly to decide what is the case about the subject at hand, one would have been led to this same set of judgments. If, as is likely, this attempt to come up with such principles is not successful, one must decide how to respond to the divergence between these principles and considered judgments: whether to give up the judgments that the principles fail to account for, to modify the principles, in hopes of achieving a better fit, or to do some combination of these things. One is then to continue in this way, working back and forth between principles and judgments, until one reaches a set of principles and a set of judgments that "account for them." This state is what Rawls calls reflective equilibrium. It should be emphasized that this is not a state Rawls believes we are currently in, or likely to reach. It is rather an ideal, the struggle to attain which "continues indefinitely."[14]

Rawls sometimes described this method as if it were a process for arriving at a description of one's beliefs about a certain subject matter—a process of characterizing our "sense of justice," as he once put it in rather

13. In "Outline of a Decision Procedure for Ethics," Rawls said that the considered judgments with which it begins are judgments concerning particular cases. But he later broadened the set of such judgments to include those judgments of any level of generality that seem evidently correct. See "The Independence of Moral Theory," p. 289.

14. *Political Liberalism*, p. 97. In "Reply to Habermas," Rawls says that reflective equilibrium is "a point at infinity we can never reach, though we may get closer to it in the sense that through discussion, our ideals, principles, and judgments seem more reasonable to us and we regard them as better founded than they were before" (*Political Liberalism*, p. 385).

psychological terms.[15] I understand the method, however, not as a process of describing what one thinks but a method for deciding what *to* think. This makes better sense of the stages of the process at which one decides whether to revise or abandon what were previously one's "considered judgments." If one were just seeking an accurate description of one's existing views, modifying these views to make them fit a proposed description would be fudging the data. Rawls's idea, as I will understand him, is rather that seeing what principles would or would not account for a given judgment may lead us to change our mind about that judgment and to reassess the reasons why it might have seemed plausible. As Rawls said about the search for principles of justice:

> Moral philosophy is Socratic: we may want to change our present considered judgments once their regulative principles are brought to light. And we may want to do this even though these principles are a perfect fit. A knowledge of these principles may suggest further reflections that lead us to revise our judgments.[16]

Why look for more general principles that would "account for" our considered judgments? I can think of at least three reasons (there may be more). First, as I have mentioned, we may have reason to want an overall account of the subject matter in question. Such an account could provide some assurance that at least some questions about the subject matter have determinate answers. It might also provide a basis for defending more specific principles (such as axioms). Second, even if such an overall account is not to be found, the process of seeking reflective equilibrium might lead to the discovery of intermediate-level principles that would help to answer questions that are not settled by our current considered judgments. Third, finding general principles that account for our considered judgments may cast new interpretive light on those judgments themselves, making clearer what they come to and why they might seem plausible.

There is, of course, no guarantee that this method, applied to a given subject, will yield general principles accounting for our considered judgments about it, let alone a convincing overall account of that subject. It might yield such an overall account, or lead only to a diverse set of partial principles. It might, however, yield no general principles, or even lead to incompatible but equally justified overall accounts of the

---

15. *A Theory of Justice*, p. 46.   16. *A Theory of Justice*, p. 49.

subject, thus supporting a kind of pluralism about the subject. In the case of set theory, for example, it might turn out that there are two ways of understanding the idea of a set, one of which supports the truth of the Continuum Hypothesis while the other does not.[17]

Suppose, however, that the application of this method to a given subject does lead to a set of general principles and considered judgments that are in "reflective equilibrium." Why should the fact that a judgment is among our judgments in such an equilibrium mean that we are justified in accepting that judgment? First, it should be emphasized that the fact that we have attained consistency by arriving at a coherent set of judgments is not itself what matters. Mere consistency among our judgments (what might be called "unreflective equilibrium") can be attained too easily, simply by throwing out conflicting judgments in one way or another. The justificatory force, if any, of being among the beliefs we have arrived at in reflective equilibrium must lie in the details of how the equilibrium is reached.

This can be seen by considering the significance of the possibility that different people, applying this method about the same subject, may reach different reflective equilibria. If we learn that someone else has reached reflective equilibrium in her beliefs about a subject involving different beliefs from ours, the fact that this person's beliefs are in equilibrium is not what matters. What is important, rather, is the way in which this equilibrium was reached. The questions to ask in such a case are, first, "Did this person reach different conclusions than I because she began with different considered judgments than I did?" If so, should I accept those different judgments? Second, "Did the person reach a different conclusion because she considered different principles than I did, or made different choices than I did about whether to revise a principle or modify a judgment that conflicts with it?" If so, should I have made these different choices as well?[18]

If the answers to these questions are positive, then we should change our beliefs, to align with this other person's. If the answers are negative, then the fact that this person has reached reflective equilibrium gives us no reason to change what we think. But there are two other possibilities.[19] One is that the plausibility of the lines of thinking leading to these divergent equilibria should lead us to suspend judgment, at least temporarily, on the questions on which we disagree. (The appropriateness of suspending judgment in this way depends on a substantive assessment of the lines of thinking leading to these two equilibria, not just on the fact that the persons reaching them are, in general, "epistemic peers."[20])

Suspending judgment in this way is compatible with continuing to believe, in the light of our overall conception of the subject at hand, that there are determinate answers to these questions, which can be disclosed by further thinking. It is also compatible with suspending judgment as to whether this is the case. The final possibility, however, is that the best explanation of the plausibility of different answers to these particular questions is that they flow from different overall accounts of this subject matter, and that the subject in question can equally well be understood in either of these two ways. This conclusion would be a pluralism of the kind that Peter Koellner describes as a possibility in the case of set theory.[21]

But even if this process leads not to pluralism of this kind but to a single set of judgments and principles, it may still be asked why we should regard the justification provided by the fact that a judgment has survived this process as sufficient justification. To answer, we need first to clarify the question: sufficient for what?

Since the method of reflective equilibrium is being put forward as the method that an individual should use in deciding what to think about a subject, one answer might be "sufficient to make the person's beliefs subjectively rational"—that is, to make it the case that the person is not open to criticism for holding these beliefs, or for the way in which he or she went about deciding whether to hold them, given the limits of his or her epistemological situation.

Although an assessment of this kind can be made from a third-person point of view, it is a subjective assessment insofar as it is relative to the epistemic situation of the person being assessed:

---

19. I am grateful to Simon Rippon for pressing me to distinguish these last two possibilities.

20. Thus, in regard to cases of disagreement between epistemic peers, I am in agreement with Thomas Kelly's Total Evidence View, and also with Derek Parfit. See Kelly, "Peer Disagreement and Higher Order Evidence," and Parfit, *On What* Matters, Volume Two, p. 428.

21. See Koellner, "Truth in Mathematics: The Question of Pluralism."

relative, that is, to the information available to that person and the questions a person in her position could be expected to think of in deciding what to believe. But such an assessment also includes objective elements. Someone making a judgment of subjective rationality must make a judgment, applying his or her own standards, about what a person in a certain epistemic situation *should have* thought of, and about what it is reasonable to conclude taking into account (only) the factors that a person in that situation should have been aware of.

So if the method of reflective equilibrium is to be understood as a standard of subjective rationality, then in determining whether a person has met this standard in forming certain beliefs we should ask whether the beliefs the person took as "considered judgments" were ones that the person had no good reason to doubt and whether, in carrying out subsequent steps of the process he or she made decisions that were reasonable (taking into account the limits of his or her epistemic situation).

A more objective assessment would drop this relativity to a person's limited epistemic situation, and address the question of when beliefs are rationally justified, *simpliciter*. As I indicated above, this is the standard we should apply in deciding how to react to the fact that someone else has reached a reflective equilibrium containing judgments that differ from our own. It is also the outlook we take in employing the method of reflective equilibrium ourselves. So, for example, in deciding whether to count a belief among our considered judgments, the question we ask is whether it is something that it is reasonable to believe, and we will answer this question in the affirmative if it *seems* reasonable to believe this and there is, as far as we can see at the outset, no reason to doubt this appearance. If there is no such reason, then we cannot be faulted for starting with these beliefs, according to either "objective" or "subjective" standards. (And if there is no such reason that we could be expected to be aware of then we at least cannot be faulted "subjectively.") Something similar holds as well for the decisions we make in subsequent steps of the process of seeking reflective equilibrium: we should ask whether there is more reason to revise a principle or to give up the judgment that conflicts with it. And we can be faulted just in case we get this wrong (or get it wrong in ways we should have been aware of).

All of this supports the conclusion that the justificatory force of the fact that we have arrived at certain judgments in reflective equilibrium depends on the substantive merits of the judgments we make along the way, in beginning with certain considered judgments and in modifying these judgments and others as we progress. I do not think this is anything that a defender of the method of reflective equilibrium should deny, or be embarrassed by. But critics often take it to be an objection to the method, or a problem for it, that conclusions it reaches are justified only if the considered judgments with which it begins are, as they put it, justified in some way other than by the method itself.[22] This is sometimes put by saying that the justificatory force of the method depends on the credibility of the considered judgments with which the process begins, not just the credence attached to these judgments by the person carrying out the process.[23]

As I hope is clear from what I have said, this way of putting the matter rests on a misunderstanding of the method itself, and in particular a misunderstanding of what it is for something to be a considered judgment. In order for something to count as a considered judgment about some subject matter it is not enough that that judgment be very confidently held. It is necessary also that it should be something that seems to me to be clearly true *when I am thinking about the matter under good conditions for arriving at judgments of the kind in question.* My belief, sitting in my armchair with no information about conditions on the moon, that there is a rock there with my name on it, does not count as a considered judgment in the required sense, no matter how certain I may be that it is true.

Making this aspect of the method explicit does not, I believe, expose a weakness in the method. But it does help to locate more clearly what is controversial about claims made for its application. Goodman, Rawls, and other advocates of the method have offered it as a way of arriving at justified beliefs about subjects that do not seem to be "underwritten by perception"—subjects such as justice, morality, logic or, in the case I have been discussing, set theory.[24] A crucial move in these claims is that we have reason to believe the things that seem to us to be true

22. See Richard Brandt, *A Theory of the Good and the Right*, p. 20; Simon Rippon, *An Epistemological Argument for Moral Response-Dependence*; Thomas Kelly and Sarah McGrath, "Is Reflective Equilibrium Enough?"; Timothy Williamson, *The Philosophy of Philosophy*, pp. 244–6.

23. See Brandt, *A Theory of the Good and the Right*; Rippon, *An Epistemological Argument for Moral Response-Dependence*.

24. As Kelly and McGrath point out in "Is Reflective Equilibrium Enough?," p. 352.

about these subjects when we are thinking about them under the right conditions, and hence that it is appropriate for us to treat these beliefs as considered judgments in a process of seeking reflective equilibrium if we have no apparent reason to doubt them. To claim that this is so in the case of beliefs about sets, or about reasons for action, is to reject the idea that there is a problem about these beliefs because, like the belief I imagined that my name is written on some rock on the moon, they have not been formed by my being "in touch with" these facts in the right way—that is, through some causal process. I made this rejection explicit in my discussion of set theory. I tried to defend it both by calling into question the metaphysical picture on which the objection seems to me to depend (this was what I called the negative component of a response to Mackie's objection), and, earlier in this lecture, by trying to make clear how the kind of thinking involved in arriving at considered judgments about sets is not a mysterious form of perception (part of the positive component of such a response).[25]

So deciding to treat something as a considered judgment involves deciding that the fact that is seems true under certain conditions is ground for treating it, at least provisionally, as being true. This may seem to suggest that all the justificatory work is done at this initial stage, before the process of seeking equilibrium has begun, and that there is little if anything left for the method of reflective equilibrium itself to do. Thus Kelly and McGrath write, "the interesting part of the story concerns not the pursuit of equilibrium itself but rather what makes it the case that certain starting points are more reasonable than others, and how we manage to recognize or grasp such facts."[26]

I think that Kelly and McGrath are correct that this is where much of the controversy about reflective equilibrium lies. That is, that much of the criticism of the method involves the allegation that it neglects the need to show "how we manage to recognize or grasp the facts" that our considered judgments are about. But their suggestion still seems to me misleading on several counts.

First, deciding to treat something as a considered judgment (and assessing objections to doing so of the kind we have been considering)

25. I am thus not trying to "evade" these problems if that means ignoring them and hoping that readers will not notice this. See Kelly and McGrath, "Is Reflective Equilibrium Enough?," p. 353. Rawls also explicitly argues against the need for causal contact in the case of judgments about justice. See *Political Liberalism*, Lecture III, Section 6.
26. Kelly and McGrath, "Is Reflective Equilibrium Enough?," p. 353.

is not something separate from the method of reflective equilibrium but, as I have emphasized, a crucial part of carrying out that method.

Second, one thing one needs to ask, in deciding whether something that seems true should be treated as a considered judgment, is whether it has any implausible implications or presuppositions. Identifying something as a *considered* judgment involves reaching a preliminary conclusion that this is not the case. Subsequent stages in the method involve testing to see whether this preliminary conclusion was correct by considering what general principles would account for that judgment. If a considered judgment survives this further examination this adds to its status as something to be believed.

Third, even though equilibrium itself (the consistency of one's set of beliefs) is of limited importance, finding general principles that account for one's beliefs has important benefits. As I said above, an overall account of a subject matter can provide assurance that some judgments about it have determinate truth values. And even if such an overall account is not to be found, finding general principles that account for our considered judgments can cast new light on those judgments themselves, making clearer what they come to and why they should seem plausible. So even though equilibrium in itself is not important, and whether or not we reach it, the *process of pursuing* reflective equilibrium, which involves identifying our considered judgments, learning more about them, and perhaps modifying them in the process of considering principles that would account for them, is the way "we manage to recognize or grasp" facts of the relevant kind. It is thus an interesting part of the story—indeed, it is the story itself.

4. Turning now from these remarks about reflective equilibrium and about the philosophy of set theory to the topic of practical reasoning that is my main concern in these lectures, let me sum up the points made so far that I believe carry over to the latter topic. I have tried to make plausible the following claims. First, there is no problem about our knowledge of sets arising from the question of how we could "be in touch with" such entities. Such a problem, if there is one, would have to be a problem about the soundness of our substantive reasoning about sets. Second, this reasoning (the reasoning supporting particular axioms and more general claims such as the Iterative Conception) depends on particular claims about sets that, while not conceptual truths, seem obviously true. It then moves from these to other claims

that are justified by the fact that they explain these claims and unify them in plausible ways. Insofar as there is room for skepticism here it must take the form of substantive challenges to the correctness of these basic claims. Third, a general account of the domain of sets, such as that offered by the Iterative Conception, is itself a piece of set theory rather than a characterization of the universe of sets in some other terms. Finally, the question of whether set theory is "objectively true independently of us" is not a metaphysical question about whether sets are part of the world, but a question about whether the domain of sets can be characterized in such a way as to support the idea that every set-theoretic statement, or at least many set-theoretic statements, have definite truth values, whether or not we could ever carry out the reasoning required to determine what these truth values actually are.

There are important differences between set theory and practical reasoning. The subject matter of set theory is an abstract theoretical domain, which can be characterized, at least partially, in a way that makes it possible to reason about it in a precise and formal manner. The subject matter of practical reasoning is, as the name implies, practical, and it is much less precise, perhaps incapable of being rendered more so. Moreover, as I will argue, it is much less plausible than in the case of set theory to hope that this domain can be characterized in such a way as to support the claim that every normative statement has a definite truth value.

I do not mean to minimize these differences. But I believe that, despite these great differences, a number of the points I have just made about our knowledge of sets carry over to the case of practical reasons. The first of these points is that, insofar as there is a problem about how we can come to know truths about reasons, this is not a problem about how we could "be in touch with" facts of the relevant kind. Nothing in the nature of normative truths suggests that these would be facts "at some distance from us," which could be perceived only through some mysterious form of intuition. The question whether something is a reason is a question we can understand and think about in familiar ways. Some conclusions we reach in these ways seem clearly to be true. For example, it seems clearly true that the fact that some action is necessary to avoid serious physical pain is, in most circumstances, a reason to do it, and it seems clearly true that if a person has reason to bring about a certain end, then the fact that some action is necessary to achieve that end is, other things equal, a reason to do it. Even these clear truths are, of course, uncertain at the edges. It is less clear exactly when pain is worth bearing, and when the fact that an action would promote an end of ours is not a reason, or not a sufficient reason, to do that thing.

Despite these uncertainties, however, there are central cases in which judgments about reasons seem clearly true. If we should reject these judgments, this has to be on the basis of substantive grounds for thinking them mistaken; not on the basis of questions about how we could be in touch with such facts at all.[27] General doubts of the latter kind would be relevant only if normative conclusions could have the significance they claim only if the facts they purport to represent had some special metaphysical character that would make them inaccessible to us. I see no more reason to believe this in the case of conclusions about practical reasons than in the case of truths about sets.

Even if this conclusion is accepted, however, it is purely negative—the rejection of a particular challenge to claims to knowledge about practical reasons. A successful rebuttal of this challenge provides, by itself, no positive assurance that claims about reasons for action in general have determinate truth values, let alone a general account of how we can know what these values are.

The second point that carries over from the our discussion of set theory is that what would, if we could get it, provide assurance of this kind would be a very general characterization of the domain of practical reasons in normative terms, analogous to one of the general characterizations of the realm of sets that I have mentioned. Such a characterization of the domain of practical reasons might provide a basis on which to argue for general principles, analogous to axioms, which could then be used to support more specific claims about reasons. And even if it did not provide such means for determining what reasons we have (or if those means were incomplete) such an account might describe the realm of practical reasons in a way that provided some assurance that claims about reasons have determinate truth values, even if we cannot always discover what they are.

What I called in my first lecture a normative desire theory would be a general characterization of the domain of practical reasons of this kind. A normative desire theory is not a naturalistic thesis, but a very general normative claim assigning normative significance to certain

---

27. Here I am in agreement with Ronald Dworkin that only internal skepticism is worth worrying about. See *Justice for Hedgehogs*, Chapter 3, esp. pp. 67–8.

natural facts, including facts about an agent's desires. It is therefore not in itself a response to metaphysical and epistemological objections to normative truths of the kind that Mackie and others have raised. But I have argued in the intervening lectures that these objections are without merit, and it would be a mistake to reject a normative desire theory on this basis. Such a theory, if it were defensible, would be just what we need.

The third point that carries over from our discussion of set theory is that in order to be defensible, a general characterization of the realm of practical reasons, such as a normative desire theory, would need to be supported by a reflective equilibrium argument: it would need to lead to plausible consequences about what we have reason to do (and not to implausible ones), and it would need to explain these consequences, and other features of practical reasons, in a plausible and illuminating way.[28] Unfortunately, desire theories do neither of these things.

Consider, first, an actual desire theory, according to which we have reason to do something if doing it would promote the fulfillment of one of our desires. Such a theory has implausible implications about the reasons we have. If I were to have a desire to walk to Alaska, this in itself would give me no reason to try to do so. It might be replied that the fact that I want to do this does give me *some* reason to do it, but the great effort and sacrifice required to do it so obviously outweigh this reason that we are led to say (mistakenly) that I have *no* reason.

But this reply is not convincing. When we engage in the kind of balancing of reasons just mentioned, what we weigh against the cost and difficulty of such a walk is not something about the desire itself—such as how intense it is—but rather the considerations that the person who has that desire sees as counting in favor of making the trek, such as visiting new parts of the country, or accomplishing something very strenuous and demanding, or the satisfaction he would feel from having done such a thing.[29]

This brings out the important point that the problem with normative (actual) desire theory is not just that it leads to implausible conclusions about the reasons people have in particular cases but that it

28. This would respond to the objection, which I mentioned in Lecture 1, that normative desire theory by itself does not provide an answer to epistemological worries about normative truth.

29. See Joseph Raz, "Incommensurability and Agency," pp. 46–66, esp. pp. 50–62.

misdescribes the relation between desires and reasons from an agent's own point of view. Having a desire to do something typically involves thinking, or imagining, that there is something to be said for doing it. And from the point of view of an agent it is the considerations that are seen as desirable, rather than the fact of having the desire, that provide reasons for acting.[30]

The situation here is analogous to the case of Naïve Set Theory. I said that Naïve Set Theory is not only to be rejected because of its consequences (which are in that case not merely implausible but contradictory), but also because it rests on a mistaken view about the relations of priority between a set, its members, and a predicate that picks these members out. Naïve Set Theory seems appealing when we focus on the idea of the *extension* of a predicate. This idea makes a set dependent on the predicates that defines it, and neglects the relation of priority between a set and its members. That relation is central to the idea of a set as a *collection*, which is expressed in the Iterative Conception. It is not that either of these ideas is incoherent (although in order to formulate the idea of sets as extensions in a way that avoids contradiction care needs to be exercised about the range of eligible predicates). The point rather is that the idea of an extension and that of a collection are different notions, and that the latter is the one more suited to the role that sets play in mathematics.

Similarly, an actual desire theory seems plausible when we focus on the explanatory question, of what an agent's reason was for doing a certain thing. This is a psychological question about the agent, a question about what the agent *saw* as a reason for acting that way (what I call the agent's "operative reason"[31]). It is natural to answer such a question by citing a psychological state, such as by saying, "He went to St. Louis because he had a desire to see the Mississippi." Citing a desire in this way does partially identify what the agent saw as a reason for acting: in this case it was something that seemed to him desirable about seeing the Mississippi. It is also true that if the agent had not had this desire he would probably not have gone to St. Louis for this reason. So the psychological facts about what his (operative) reason for going was depend on facts about his desires. This may be one thing that has

---

30. I argue for this view of desires in *What We Owe to Each Other*, pp. 37 ff. See also Warren Quinn, "Putting Rationality in its Place," pp. 236, 246–7; and Joseph Raz, *The Morality of Freedom*, pp. 140–3.

31. *What We Owe to Each Other*, p. 19.

seemed to support a normative desire theory. But it does not actually support such a theory, since it deals only with the psychological question of an agent's operative reasons rather that with what reasons an agent has in the normative sense. (In addition, as pointed out above, from the agent's own point of view what provides his reason is not his desire but features of the object of this desire.)

So far, this idea of a reason lying behind actual desire theory is entirely psychological and explanatory rather than normative. A normative element may seem to be added, however, by an appeal to rationality—to the thought that it is rational to act on one's desires. This idea is strengthened by taking into account the fact just mentioned that having a desire involves seeing certain considerations as reasons. If having a desire involves seeing something as a reason to pursue the object of that desire, then as long as one does not reject this desire—as long as one continues to see oneself as having this reason— it is irrational to deny that one has a reason to do what will promote the attainment of this object.[32]

This line of thinking confuses the normative question, "What does someone in this situation have reason to do?" with the question of rationality, "What must a person, insofar as he is not irrational, see as a reason for doing *a*, given his other present attitudes?" These questions are easily confused, but they are distinct. And it is the former question, rather than either the explanatory question (of what was a person's reason for acting) or the question of rationality, that a normative desire theory is supposed to be answering.

These problems are not avoided by shifting to an ideal desire theory, which holds that one has reason to do what would fulfill the desires one would have (for one in one's present situation) under ideal conditions in which one was fully informed, thinking clearly, and so on. This is shown when we ask why what a person would desire under these ideal conditions is supposed to be relevant to what he or she should do now. If the answer is that these are conditions under which the person is most likely to get things right, normatively speaking, then what we have is no longer a desire theory. What is playing the fundamental role is not desires but the normative facts that one's desires under ideal

---

32. Bernard Williams' internalist view involves both of these elements: the idea that reasons must be able to explain an agent's actions and also, as I argued, in Lecture 1, the idea that it is irrational to reject claims about reasons that follow by "a sound deliberative route" from one's desires and other elements of one's "subjective motivational set."

conditions would be responsive to. Alternatively, one might say that what a person would want (for herself now) under ideal conditions is relevant because it indicates what would in fact best promote that person's present desires, when best understood. This interpretation clings to the rationality-based line of thinking that I discussed above, and retains the weakness of that line of thought: it delivers only conclusions about what an agent must, insofar as he or she is not irrational, recognize as a reason *given* his or her present desires, rather than conclusions about what that person actually has reason to do.

If normative desire theories are to be rejected, this leaves us with the question of whether there is some other general characterization of the domain of reasons that would provide a basis for substantive principles of practical reasoning and give some assurance that at least some questions about reasons for action have determinate answers. The main candidates for this role seem to me to be some form of constructivism or some (other) way of grounding reasons in an idea of rationality. I will try to explain why neither of these seems to me likely to succeed.

5. A constructivist account of a subject characterizes the facts about that subject by specifying some procedure through which these facts are determined, or "constructed." Many quite different accounts fit this broad definition. The reasons why a process of construction might seem a particularly good way of providing an account with the two advantages just mentioned will vary, depending on the domain in question.

Constructivism in mathematics is a response to concerns about characterizations of a domain in terms of a "completed infinite" such as "the set containing 0 and closed under successor." The worry is that such a characterization does not guarantee that all statements about the domain have determinate truth values. Some constructivists maintain, for example, that in order to establish that for every number, x, there is a number, y, such that $M(x, y)$, it is not sufficient to derive a contradiction from the assumption that for some n, not-$M(n, m)$ for every m. This conclusion would depend on what constructivists regard as the unwarranted assumption that it is either true or false that (x) $\exists y M(x, y)$. What is required to establish such a conclusion, they say, is to provide a procedure through which, given any n, we can find an m such that $M(n, m)$.

The Iterative Conception of Set is not a constructivist account in this sense, because the transfinite construction it involves is not one that we could carry out. But it is constructivist in the more general sense I described. The construction it describes seems an appropriate way to characterize the realm of sets insofar as it seems to capture the idea that a set is an arbitrary collection of independently existing objects. If this is what sets are then it seems plausible that the universe of sets will contain just those that can be "built up" out of whatever elements we begin with. The question we need to consider is why a process of construction should seem an appropriate way to characterize a normative domain.

The answer I will explore is that a constructivist account of a normative domain is appealing because it seems to offer a way of explaining how normative judgments can have determinate truth values that are independent of us while also providing a basis for our epistemological access to these truths and an explanation of their practical significance for us. It thus responds to the tensions lying behind Mackie's challenge: the tension between the independence of these truths from us and our knowledge of them, and the tension between their independence of us and their practical significance for us (their "prescriptivity").

To see how a constructivist account might do this, consider first the account offered by John Rawls, who introduced the term "constructivism" in this area.[33] Rawls was concerned not with normativity in general or with morality in general but with justice, that is to say, principles for the assessment of basic social institutions. The function of such principles, he believed, is to serve as a shared basis for assessing conflicting claims from citizens about what their institutions should be like. The main conflicts of this kind, he thought, will be between individuals in different economic classes and between individuals who have different religious views or, more generally, different "conceptions of the good." So principles appropriate for this mediating role need to be justified on a basis that individuals on both sides of these disagreements have reason to accept. Rawls suggested that principles would have this kind of justification if they would be agreed to by parties who did not know what economic class they represented or what

---

33. See Rawls, "Kantian Constructivism in Moral Theory," and *Political Liberalism*, Lecture III, "Political Constructivism."

conception of the good they held. He made this idea more precise in his idea of an Original Position in which principles of justice are to be chosen.[34]

The resulting theory, that the correct principles of justice are ones that would be agreed to by parties in the Original Position Rawls described, has the form of a constructivist view: it holds that facts about justice are facts about what principles would be arrived at through a process of a certain kind. Even though Rawls' Original Position is defined quite clearly, carrying out his constructivist procedure requires the exercise of judgment about what principles of justice individuals in such a position would have reason to choose. The account remains constructivist because the judgments in question are not judgments about what is just or unjust (or morally right or wrong) but rather judgments about individual practical rationality—about what individuals who are seeking only to do as well for themselves as they can would have reason to choose under conditions of limited knowledge. Rawls' case for this constructivist account of justice lies ultimately with a reflective equilibrium argument. His claim is that this account fits with what are, on reflection, our considered judgments about justice and provides a satisfying explanation of these judgments.

The fact that principles would be chosen through a procedure of the kind Rawls described gives us reason to be concerned with them because it indicates that they have the kind of impartial justification that makes them fit for the role that principles of justice are supposed to play. This is only a partial explanation, since it can always be asked what reason we have to be concerned with impartial justifications of this kind. The answer is given, I believe, by pointing to the character that our relations with our fellow citizens have if we are cooperating with them on principles that have such a justification, compared with the character of these relations when our institutions cannot be justified in this way. The force of this appeal can of course be debated further. (Every justification has to start somewhere.) But because Rawls' constructivist theory of the content of justice connects with this rationale for caring about justice, it offers more than an account that consisted simply of general principles specifying what justice requires.

---

34. *A Theory of Justice*, Chapter III.

This constructivist account also provides an explanation of the objectivity of claims about justice—the sense in which they are correct or incorrect "independent of us." To assess this explanation we should consider first the various ways in which the idea of independence can be understood.

The first is the idea that a subject matter is "independent of us," and judgments about it are objective, if it is possible for us (at least individually) to be mistaken in our judgments about that subject. Call this form of objectivity *judgment-independence.* I believe that truths of arithmetic and set theory are objective in this sense. I believe this because there are ways of thinking about these questions which anyone who understands the subject can engage in, and which seem to lead clearly to certain conclusions. These "ways of thinking" need not be algorithms, although in the case of arithmetic they sometimes are. More informal methods—such as those we use to convince ourselves of many of the axioms of set theory—can suffice. Our grounds for thinking that judgments about a subject are judgment-independent lie not just in the existence of *de facto* agreement, but also the tendency of the judgments of different competent judges to converge, and the stability of our own judgments. It is important, for example, that there is such a thing as discovering errors in our thinking about the subject, and that when we conclude that something is an error this conclusion is generally stable—we do not generally flip back the other way.

I believe that facts about reasons for action are also judgment-independent. It is important however, to distinguish two different elements in this claim. The first is just that my judging that something is a reason does not make it so. Whether my judgment has this effect or not is a first-order normative question, the answer to which seems obviously to be that it does not.[35] But it is a further question whether normative claims (including this one) have determinate truth values at all. This is the question of determinateness that a general account of the normative domain could help to answer.

Judgment-independence is an important property, but it is a fairly weak form of objectivity. Even judgments about what is the case

35. A point on which expressivists such as Gibbard and Blackburn agree. See Gibbard, *Thinking How to Live,* p. 186 and Blackburn, "Errors and the Phenomenology of Value," p. 153.

according to a make-believe game can be objective in this sense, as can judgments about what is permitted by certain social norms.[36] But these things are not "independent of us" in a second, stronger sense that we often have in mind in discussing objectivity.

A subject matter is independent of us, and judgments about it are objective in a further sense, if these judgments are judgment-independent and, in addition, the standards for assessing such judgments do not depend on what we, collectively, have done, chosen, or adopted, and would not be different had we done, chosen, or adopted something else. Call this *choice-independence*. Judgments about *what is true within* a make-believe game, or what is required by a social norm, can be both judgment-independent and choice-independent. Moves in chess are legitimate or illegitimate whether chess is a game we play or not. But judgments that presuppose that we are playing one game rather than another, or have one social practice rather than another, such as judgments about "who won" or about who is "the head of a household" are not choice-independent even if they are judgment-independent.

Many mathematical judgments, such as propositions of number theory and arithmetic, seem to be objective in both of these senses. Many axioms of set theory (such as the standard Zermelo-Frankel axioms) are choice-independent as well as judgment-independent. But if "pluralism" about set theory turns out to be correct then there are further axioms of set theory that are not choice-independent: the reasons they give us to accept the conclusions that they lead to as conclusions *about sets* depend on our having chosen that particular way of developing the concept of set.[37]

I believe that many truths about reasons for action are both judgment-independent and choice-independent. There is disagreement about whether this is so. But even if truths about reasons are independent of us in both of these senses they are not all "independent of us" in the further sense of being *independent of what we are like*. If my flesh were not soft and liable to being cut, the fact that a piece of metal is sharp would not be a reason for me not to press my hand against it, and if I enjoyed different things then I would have reasons to do different

---

36. This notion of objectivity is explored by John Searle in *The Construction of Social Reality*.
37. Feferman, for example, maintains that this is so. See his "Conceptions of the Continuum."

things. It should not be troubling or surprising that *mixed* (but not pure) normative facts depend on non-normative facts about us in this way.[38]

According to Rawls' constructivist account, judgments about justice are objective in the sense of being *judgment-independent* if judgments about what parties in Rawls' Original Position have reason to choose, and judgments about what follows from those principles are judgments we can be mistaken about. This seems quite plausible. Judgments about what the parties in the Original Position would have reason to choose are a kind of normative judgment. But their objectivity is less controversial than that of many normative judgments because they are only *hypothetical* normative judgments—judgments about what parties would have reason to do *given* that they had reasons to achieve certain specified aims and given certain background information. These judgments are in this respect like judgments about games or social norms that have judgment-independence but lack choice-independence. This is not, however, a flaw from the point of view of the aims of Rawls' constructivist theory.

As I said earlier, the appeal of a constructivist theory of a normative subject lies in the promise of giving an account of that subject that supports the idea that judgments about it have determinate truth values, provides a way of finding out what these truth values are, and provides or fits with a plausible account of the practical significance of such judgments. The fact that, on Rawls' account, the determinate truth values of judgments about justice depend on the choice of a particular way of defining the Original Position is not a problem if the fact that a principle would be arrived at in a choice situation of that particular kind is a reason for us to give that principle the authority claimed for principles of justice. A claim that it does give us such a reason is an unconditional normative claim about what one has reason to do in certain circumstances, and therefore more controversial than the conditional claims about what parties in the Original Position would have reason to choose, given their aims and the information available to them. But this should not undermine the *determinateness* that judgments about justice would have on this constructivist account, even for a person who has doubts about the

---

38. What they depend on are facts about the individuals involved, not facts about what is normal for human beings.

objectivity of unconditional normative judgments, since on this account the truth values of judgments of justice depend only on the truth values of *conditional* normative judgments. What we have, then, is a two-part thesis: an account of the truth values of judgments about justice, which depends only on conditional normative claims, and an account of the significance of such judgments, which depends on unconditional claims about reasons, whose objectivity may be more controversial.

Any suggestion of arbitrariness flowing from the dependence of the truth values of judgments about justice on the choice of a particular way of defining the Original Position would be further reduced, or even eliminated, I would say, if a larger reflective equilibrium argument establishes that the account of justice provided by this definition is the one that best fits with all of our considered judgments about justice. (It is the lack of a corresponding argument that could lead to a "pluralist" view of set theory.)

My own Contractualist theory of moral right and wrong could also count as a constructivist account in the broad sense I am considering (in this case, a constructivist account of individual morality).[39] According to this account, in order to determine whether an action is morally permissible we should consider a general principle that would permit it. We then consider what objections individuals in various situations could offer to this principle based on the ways in which they would be affected by it: the ways their lives would be affected by living with the consequences of the actions it would permit and with the possibility that agents may perform such actions, since they would be permitted to do so. We then compare these reasons with the reasons that individuals would have to object to a principle that would forbid actions of the kind in question, based, again on how they would be affected by such a principle, and decide whether it would be reasonable for those who have reason to object to the principle permitting the action to reject it, given the reasons that others have for objecting to the contrary principle. If it would be reasonable to reject any principle that would permit a certain action, then that action would be morally wrong. (And the rightness or wrongness of an action depends on what the correct outcome of this procedure would be, whether or not anyone has carried it out.)

---

39. See Scanlon, *What We Owe to Each Other*, Chapters 4, 5.

Like Rawls' constructivist account of judgments about justice, this account of the subject matter of moral rightness and wrongness makes facts about this subject matter depend on facts about what principles individuals in certain circumstances would have reason to accept or reject. It then explains the practical significance of judgments about right and wrong on the ground that we have reason to care about principles that could not be rejected in this way—specifically, that we have reason to care about whether our actions are justifiable to others in this way. The case for accepting this account of rightness and wrongness then depends, as before, on a reflective equilibrium argument that it provides the best overall account of our considered judgments about this subject matter, including, as before, judgments "of all levels of generality," not just judgments about the rightness and wrongness of particular actions.

On this account, judgments of right and wrong will have a particular form of objectivity—will be judgment-independent or choice-independent—just in case judgments about what individuals in certain circumstances could reasonably reject have these forms of objectivity. In contrast to Rawls' constructivist account of justice, however, my constructivist account makes the truth values and the objectivity of moral judgments depend on fully normative judgments about reasons for action. These are judgments about what individuals in specified circumstances who, among other things, care about finding principles others could also accept, would have reason to do.

The question of present concern is whether there could be a constructivist account of *these* judgments—that is, of the general domain of facts about which things individuals in various circumstances have more reason to want to have, or to avoid. Such an account would involve a process for arriving at conclusions about whether a given consideration is or is not a reason for a person in certain circumstances to act in a certain way. For reasons mentioned above, assessing the validity of the steps in this process cannot involve making independent judgments about which things are or are not reasons for action.

If a constructivist account of reasons for action is to have ambitions parallel to those of constructivist accounts of justice and moral rightness and wrongness, the fact that the conclusion that p is a reason for a person in c to do a can be arrived at through this process should help to explain the practical significance of the fact that p is such a reason. The practical significance of judgments about justice or about moral right and wrong can be seen as lying in the fact that when such a judg-ment is correct we have *good reason* to be guided by it in deciding what to do. So in these cases practical significance can be explained in terms of reasons. But, as I argued in Lecture 1, this is not an option where judgments about reasons for action are concerned. It is nonsensical to ask what reason we have to do what we have reason to do. So if the practical significance of judgments about reasons is to be explained this must take some other form.

Finally, if a constructivist account of reasons for action is to be sup-ported in reflective equilibrium, it should seem evident that at least those judgments about reasons that seem most clearly correct are ones that could be arrived at through the procedure that this account describes.

Although I think that constructivist accounts of justice and morality have considerable plausibility, I do not believe that a plausible con-structivist account of reasons for action in general can be given. In the remainder of this lecture I will try to explain why.

The best-known attempt to provide such a view is what has come to be called Kant's Categorical Imperative procedure.[40] Kant's Cate-gorical Imperative is a test of the acceptability of maxims, which I will take to be general policies of taking certain considerations as reasons to act in certain ways. A maxim passes the Categorical Imperative test if it can be willed to be a universal law or if adopting it is consistent with regarding rational nature (whether one's own or that of another rational creature) as an end-in-itself. This is commonly understood as a test of the moral acceptability of a maxim, and of acting on such a maxim. So understood, it seems too limited to provide a general account of reasons for action since, presumably, it can be permissible for a person to do things that, as it happens, he or she has no reason to do. In Christine Korsgaard's version of the Kantian account, this gap is filled by the idea of an agent's practical identities. A practical identity is "a description under which you value yourself and find your life worth living and your actions to be worth undertaking. Conceptions of prac-tical identity include such things as roles and relationships, citizenship, memberships in ethnic or religious groups, causes, vocations, profes-sions, and offices."[41]

---

40. See Korsgaard, *The Sources of Normativity*; O'Neill, *Constructions of Reason*.
41. Korsgaard, *Self-Constitution: Agency, Identity, and Integrity*, p. 20.

The overall idea is this: insofar as we see ourselves as acting at all, we must see the Categorical Imperative as constraining our practical thought. So we have reasons characterized by the maxims that this requires us to adopt. Beyond this, we have reasons to do those things that are required by the more specific practical identities we have adopted, provided that these are compatible with the Categorical Imperative. This view can be seen as constructivist insofar as it provides a procedure through which it is determined whether something is a reason for a person: something is a reason for a person if denying that it was a reason would violate the Categorical Imperative or be inconsistent with some practical identity (consistent with the Categorical Imperative) that that person has adopted. The fact that valid judgments about reasons arise from this process is supposed to explain their practical significance: their special authority lies in the agent's own will in the fact that they flow from choices the agent has made or from an identity that an agent must endorse insofar as she sees herself as acting at all.

According to this account, judgments about reasons are judgment-independent: an individual can be mistaken about what is required by the Categorical Imperative or by some practical identity that he or she has adopted. Those judgments about reasons that follow from the Categorical Imperative itself will also be choice-independent, but reasons flowing from the practical identities that the agent has chosen will not be. Whether this is a flaw in the account, or an advantage, is something to be determined by the process of seeking reflective equilibrium in our overall judgments about reasons. It is quite plausible to say that some reasons a person has depend on prior choices he or she has made. The question is when this is true and how this dependence is best explained.[42]

I do not see how such a constructivist account of reasons can succeed. Although it seems true that individuals have different reasons depending on the ends and practical identities they have adopted, these reasons depend on their having good reasons to adopt those ends or identities in the first place, and not to revise or reject them. As Korsgaard says, we need to have "a way to say to ourselves of some ends that there are reasons for them, that they are good."[43] On her Kantian view these "unconditional reasons on which hypothetical reasons depend"

42. I discuss this question in "Reasons: A Puzzling Duality?" and in "Structural Irrationality." See also Niko Kolodny, "Aims as Reasons."
43. "The Normativity of Instrumental Reason," p. 63.

must be "grounded in autonomy," that is to say in Kant's Categorical Imperative.[44] But, despite the initial appeal of the various forms of this Imperative as principles of morality, I am not convinced by any arguments I have seen for the claim that we must see them as binding on us insofar as we see ourselves as rational agents at all.[45] Without this foundation, and given that appeal to independent substantive truths about reasons is ruled out, this constructivist procedure seems to reduce to one in which an agent's adoption of any end can, by itself, generate reasons. This would be an implausible form of bootstrapping.

If this Kantian constructivist account of reasons for action is not satisfactory, might there be another constructivist account that would be more successful? Part of the appeal of the Kantian account was that it not only promised to provide a standard for the correctness of judgments about reasons but also promised to do this in a way that explained the practical significance of these judgments by grounding facts about reasons in a conception of rational agency. So one question is whether there might be a different conception of rationality that could play this grounding role. This would have to be a conception that did not itself involve or depend on substantive claims about what reasons people have, but which led to conclusions about such claims. I do not myself see what such a conception could be. Some things that are referred to as conceptions of rationality are very general substantive theses about reasons—such as the idea that what is rational for a person is to do what is in his or her self-interest. These could not serve as an explanation of the practical significance of facts about reasons. The only non-substantive alternative that I am aware of is the formal conception of rationality discussed by John Broome and others, according to which rational requirements are simply requirements of consistency among a person's practical attitudes.[46] These requirements have no substantive implications about the reasons people have. So no account of either of these kinds would provide a basis for claims about reasons.

6. It is possible however, that there might be a constructivist account of reasons of a less ambitious kind. Such an account would keep the ambition of characterizing the domain of reasons in a way that supported the idea that judgments about reasons have determinate truth

---

44. "The Normativity of Instrumental Reason," p. 65.
45. For somewhat fuller discussion see my "How I am not a Kantian."
46. See, e.g. Broome, "Does Rationality Consist in Responding Correctly to Reasons?"

values. But it would abandon the further aim of explaining the practical significance of conclusions about reasons, resting simply with the idea that the "normative authority" of a reason is simply that—being a reason—and that this cannot be explained any further way. Such an account would be similar in its ambitions to the account of sets offered by the Iterative Conception of Set, and to a normative desire theory of reasons which, as I have said, would have significant advantages if it were correct. Might there, then, be a constructivist account of reasons of this more limited kind?

It does seem that some reasons depend on others. Roughly speaking, it seems that if a person has good reason to have a certain end, then he or she has good reason to do what will promote it, and if a person has good reason to hold a certain value, or to adopt a particular practical identity, then he or she has good reason to do what is involved in respecting this value or living in accord with this identity.[47] Most of our day-to-day thinking about reasons for action takes place within structures of this kind. We operate on the assumption that we have reason to seek certain experiences and accomplishments of certain kinds, and that certain relationships are ones we have reason to seek and to preserve. And our thinking about what we have reason to do on particular occasions is largely a matter of working out what reasons follow from ("are constructed within") this normative framework. So one might say that constructivism about reasons is *locally* true.

But this cannot be generalized into an overall account of practical reasons, because our thinking about reasons depends on too many disparate starting points that are not constructed from other reasons. It might be claimed that these starting points are not as diverse as I have claimed: that, for example, the only non-derivative reasons are reasons to avoid pain and seek pleasure, and that all other reasons are constructed out of these in ways like those just described. This would have the right kind of structure to be a global, as opposed to merely local, constructivist account of practical reasons. But it does not seem to me a very plausible proposal, because it does not seem that the only non-derivative reasons are those provided by pleasure and pain. More generally, no account of this kind seems likely to succeed: the range of non-derived elements

---

47. Exactly how this is so is a complicated matter. See Raz, "The Myth of Instrumental Rationality," and Kolodny, "Aims as Reasons."

in the domain of reasons for action is too varied to be plausibly explained by a systematic overall account. I do not have an argument for this negative conclusion, but it seems to me evident, from consideration of the candidate theories and of the diversity of the reasons that would have to be explained.

How then do we come to know particular non-derivative truths about which things are reasons? My own answer is that we do this simply by thinking carefully about what seem to us to be reasons, considering what general principles about reasons would explain them, what implications these would have, and considering the plausibility of the implications of these principles. For example, suppose it seems to me that someone has reason to do a because he or she would find it pleasant. Pleasure does not always constitute a reason (pleasure in the suffering of others, for example, does not). So we need to ask what attitudes this particular pleasure involves, and whether they are attitudes that one has reason to hold, or reason to hold in the particular circumstances in question.

One might characterize this process as one of bringing one's particular judgments about reasons and one's general principles about when something is a reason into reflective equilibrium. This seems to me broadly correct, although the distinction between particular judgments and general principles that explain them is in this case less than sharp. The process I have just described is one of coming to a clearer understanding of the conditions, c, under which some fact p is a reason. So it is a matter of clarifying what particular judgment we in fact accept, rather than a matter of finding a separate principle that "explains" this judgment.

This being noted, it seems to me that such a process of careful reflection is the only way we have of arriving at conclusions about reasons for action. If this process of seeking reflective equilibrium in our practical judgments is the only way we have of figuring out what reasons we have, might this process itself be seen as a constructivist account of the domain of reasons? Sharon Street, for example, speaks of a constructivist view according to which the truth of a judgment that $R(p, x, c, a)$ is "a function of" whether such a judgment would be among x's evaluative judgments in reflective equilibrium.[48]

---

48. Street, "A Darwinian Dilemma for Realist Theories of Value," p. 110. (I have modified Street's notation to fit the one I have been using.)

There are several problems with this proposed account. First, it is not plausible to claim that if the judgment that p is a reason for x to do a would be among x's evaluative beliefs in reflective equilibrium then p is a reason for x to a *however x carried out the process of reaching this equilibrium*.[49] There are many ways of reaching equilibrium. As I pointed out earlier, the normative status conferred on a judgment by its being in a set that is in reflective equilibrium depends on the quality of the decisions that are made in arriving at that equilibrium—decisions about what to count as a considered judgment at the outset and about what to modify in situations of conflict. So the most that could be said is that p is a reason for x to do a if the judgment that it is such a reason would be among x's evaluative judgments in reflective equilibrium *if the judgments x made in arriving at this equilibrium were sound*. So understood, however, this is not a constructivist account of reasons, since the steps involved in carrying out the process in question would involve making judgments about what is or is not a reason.

Leaving aside the applicability of the label, "constructivist," however, it is true for the same reason that "the truths about reasons are the judgments about reasons that one would reach as a result of a process of seeking reflective equilibrium, carried out in the right way" is not itself an account of the *subject matter* of practical reasons at all. In deciding whether a certain claim is among one's considered judgments, or in deciding whether to modify such a judgment in the light of its conflict with a principle one has arrived at or to modify or abandon the principle in the light of this conflict, the question one asks cannot be "Will this judgment be among those I would arrive at if I reached reflective equilibrium?" The question is rather "Is this judgment correct?" The process of seeking reflective equilibrium in one's beliefs about a subject matter is therefore not a characterization of the facts about that subject matter but rather a method for arriving at conclusions about that subject matter, of various degrees of generality.

Where does this leave us with respect to whether statements about reasons have truth values independent of us? In the case of set theory I said that assurance on this point could be provided by a substantive overall account of the realm of sets that was itself supported by a reflective equilibrium argument. I gave two examples of such accounts (both

---

49. Although this may in fact be Street's view. See her "In Defense of Future Tuesday Indifference: Ideally Coherent Eccentrics and the Contingency of What Matters."

unsuccessful) and said that although we do not at present have such an account it is possible that one may be found. In the case of practical reasons, on the other hand, I believe that such an overall account is very unlikely. We have "local" reasoning about reasons in various areas, dependent on a diverse set of normative starting points which are themselves supported by a process of seeking reflective equilibrium, and in many cases subject to fairly constant reinterpretation in the light of such a process. Our confidence that statements about reasons have determinate truth values thus depends on our confidence in the results of this process in particular cases rather than on some general account of reasons, of the sort that a normative desire theory, or a global constructivist theory, would provide.

This reflects the fact that the domain of practical reasons is not a unified subject matter like the domain of sets, the content of which we should expect to be determined by overall principles characterizing this domain. This does not mean that we should lack confidence in the particular conclusions we reach about reasons for action, but only that our confidence (often justified) is a matter of confidence in those particular conclusions rather than a general confidence that all questions about reasons have determinate answers, whether we have reached them or not.

Lecture 5

Reasons and their Strength

1. The questions about reasons that I listed in my first lecture included the following two:

Strength: Reasons have varying strengths. The reason to turn the wheel of the car in order to avoid hitting a pedestrian, for example, is a stronger reason than the reason to go on listening to enjoyable music. What is strength, and how do we determine the strength of different reasons?

Optionality: Some reasons seem to be "optional"—merely reasons it makes sense to act on if one chooses—whereas other reasons are normatively conclusive—reasons it does not make sense *not* to act on. How should this difference be understood?

In this final lecture I will address these questions in the light of the relational view of reasons that I have advanced. I have so far been discussing the weakest normative relation, $R(p, x, c, a)$, understood as the minimal claim that, for an agent in circumstances, c, p counts in favor of doing a. This claim leaves entirely open whether p is a conclusive reason that should settle the matter of whether to do a, or whether it is even a sufficient reason for doing a under the circumstances—whether it would be reasonable to do a for that reason under these conditions. The claim that $R(p, x, c, a)$ holds is just the claim that p is a consideration that it would be proper to take into account, as something counting in favor of a, in considering what to do in those circumstances.

The claim that $R(p, x, c, a)$ holds does entail a claim of one kind about the normative force of other considerations in c, namely that these considerations do not undercut p as a reason to do a. A consideration q that holds in c *undercuts* p as a reason to do a in c if it is not the case that $R(p, x, c, a)$ but it is the case that $R(p, x, c', a)$ where c' is a situation as normatively similar to c as possible in which p holds and q does not. To go beyond the idea of undercutting, and to capture the idea of one consideration's being a stronger reason than another and the idea of a reason's being optional, we need to consider normative relations that are stronger than R.

As a first step, consider the relation $SR(p, x, c, a)$, which holds just in case p is a sufficient reason for doing a in circumstances c. When this relation holds, a person who does a in c for this reason is not open to rational criticism for taking p to be sufficient reason to do a, whether or not there are other considerations in c that count in favor of doing a.[1] Even if it is true that $SR(p, x, c, a)$, however, it can also be true that a person who was aware of this would not be open to rational criticism for failing to do a. So doing a in c for reason p is optional.

But this idea of optionality leaves open the possibility that a person in c who, knowing that it is the case that p, fails to respond to this as a reason for doing a is not liable to rational criticism only because there is some "counterbalancing" factor, q, in c, such that $SR(q, x, c, b)$, where b is a course of action incompatible with doing a.

The reason that I mentioned at the beginning of this lecture as being optional—the pleasure of listening to some music on the radio— seems to be optional in a stronger sense. It makes sense for me to listen to some music for this reason, but even if I know this I do not have to have some countervailing reason for not turning on the radio in order not to be open to rational criticism to failing to turn it on. Things might be different if, for example, a friend's performance was being broadcast.

It should not seem mysterious that many reasons are optional in this stronger sense. There is, at any given moment, a vast range of things that I would have sufficient reason to do, and in order not to be open to rational criticism I do not have to have countervailing reasons for not responding to each of them, or even to each of the reasons that I am aware of. This would not be possible if the reasons that one has in a certain situation each had, as it were, a certain normative force under these conditions, and if being rational were a matter of doing what is supported by the resolution of these normative forces. If that were so, then reasons could still be "optional" in the weaker sense I mentioned:

---

1. The agent might still be open to rational criticism for failure to see that he or she also had some *other* reason for doing a. For example, she might see, correctly, that p, a reason of self-interest, was sufficient reason to do a, but fail to see that the moral objections to failing to do a gave her equally strong reasons for doing a. I am grateful to Alex Voorhoeve for calling this to my attention.

if two reasons for incompatible courses of action were of equal force then it could be rational to do either of these things. But there could be no optional reasons in the stronger sense I am now considering. If a consideration is one that it makes sense to act on in a given situation, then on the view just described it does not make sense *not* to act on it unless some countervailing reason for doing something else is present.

This model of rational decision-making seems to me mistaken. Reasons can render an action rationally eligible without making it rationally required in the absence of some countervailing reason. Being rational involves not only identifying and assessing the reasons one has, but also selecting courses of action from among those that one has sufficient reason to do.[2] It therefore seems possible that some reasons, such as my reason to turn on the radio to hear some music, can be optional in the stronger sense. It is, however, slightly misleading to refer to these as optional reasons. Reasons themselves are not optional: a consideration is a reason in a certain situation or it is not. What is optional is acting on certain reasons.[3]

I have so far been considering questions about the normative standing of particular considerations, such as whether a given consideration is sufficient reason for an action in certain circumstances, and whether acting on it may be optional. It is appropriate to focus on a particular consideration, *p*, in this way, distinguishing it from normatively significant considerations included in the background conditions, *c*, when we are concerned with the relation, R—that is, with whether a consideration counts in favor of acting in a certain way in certain circumstances. But when we turn to stronger normative relations such as SR(*p, x, c, a*) it may seem that the relevant question is not whether some given consideration, *p*, is sufficient reason for a certain action but simply whether an agent in those circumstances *has sufficient reason* (or even conclusive reason) to act in that way. An agent in certain circumstances might have sufficient reason to do *a* even though in that situation no particular consideration, *p*, considered on its own, was sufficient reason to do *a* in the narrower sense I defined above: that is, it is not

---

2. Here I am in agreement with what Joseph Raz calls the classical model of rational agency. See Raz, "Incommensurability and Agency," pp. 47–9.

3. I take Joseph Raz to be asserting a similar view when he says, "They [reasons] are not optional in themselves, but they are optional in the circumstances. They render options attractive, make their choice intelligible, but they do not make it unreasonable, let alone wrong, not to choose them" (*Engaging Reason*, p. 103).

true of any of these particular considerations that a person would not be open to rational criticism for doing a for that reason regardless of whether there were any other considerations in that situation counting in favor of doing a.

But we do sometimes ask whether particular reasons are sufficient in this sense. We may ask, for example, whether the fact that I would find it amusing to do something is sufficient reason to do it in a given situation or, more strongly, whether the fact that I promised to do something is, in a certain situation, conclusive reason to do the thing promised. So I will continue to understand the relation $SR(p, x, c, a)$ in this narrower way, as holding whenever p is by itself a sufficient reason for doing a, leaving aside whatever other reasons there may be, in the circumstances, for doing so. And I will adopt a similar understanding of the relation, $CR(p, x, c, a)$, which holds when p is a conclusive reason for doing a in c. Understanding SR in this way, we might define the relation of outweighing as follows:

One consideration, q, outweighs another, p, if the following hold: $R(p, x, c, a)$, $R(q, x, c, b)$, where b is a course of action incompatible with a, and $SR(q, x, c, b)$ but not $SR(p, x, c, a)$, although $SR(p, x, c', a)$ where c' is a set of circumstances as normatively similar to c as possible except that q does not obtain in c'.

When q outweighs p in this sense, it is natural to say that q is a stronger reason than p. This does not capture all that might intuitively be meant by strength, however. It does not, for example, cover claims about the relative strength of two considerations as reasons for the same action. For example, the fact that my friends who are giving a party will be hurt if I do not appear may be a stronger reason for going to the party than the fact that the food will be good. We might say that this idea of strength is represented by the fact that the quality of the food would not be sufficient reason to go to the party if my friends would be hurt by my going. More generally, such cases of relative strength might be captured by saying that p is stronger than q as a reason for doing a in circumstances c if there is some consideration r, which is a reason for doing some b that is incompatible with doing a, such that r outweighs q but does not outweigh p.[4] This counterfactual interpretation may, however, seem indirect, and not to capture the full intuitive idea of strength. I will return to this question.

---

4. Joshua Gert proposes a counterfactual criterion of strength of this kind in "Normative Strength and the Balance of Reasons," p. 538.

Another objection to this proposed definition is that it may seem not to capture the relation of priority between the strength of reasons and relations such as outweighing. It does not, the objection holds, reflect the fact that one consideration outweighs another *because* it is a stronger reason, or the fact that we arrive at conclusions about whether a consideration is a sufficient reason for acting a certain way by comparing its strength with that of competing considerations.

This idea, that strength is an independent property of individual reasons, might be expressed by saying that the basic normative relation is actually a five-place relation ("the fact that p, is a reason of strength s for an agent x, in circumstances c, to do a)." These strengths, it is argued, explain relations of outweighing and conclusions about when reasons are sufficient or conclusive. The question is how this idea of strength is to be understood.

The idea that reasons, considered on their own, have such a property of strength may derive its plausibility from certain substantive accounts of reasons for action. Consider, for example, a desire-based theory of reasons, which holds that an agent has a reason for doing a only if doing a would satisfy some desire that he or she has. Such a view might hold that the strength of a reason corresponds to the motivational strength of the desire that backs it.[5] Given relevant facts about agents' desires, this theory would assign degrees of strength to all reasons, including to reasons for the same action as well as competing reasons for different actions. Another version of a desire theory would be a utility-based account, which held that agents have reason to do what promotes the satisfaction of their preferences, and that the strength of a consideration as a reason for action consists in the increase in the agent's utility (or expected utility) that that consideration indicates the proposed action would lead to.

The strength of reasons might be explained in a similar way by a hedonistic theory, which held that reasons for action are provided, ultimately, by the balance of pleasure over pain that those actions would produce, and that the strength of some consideration as a reason for action lies in the balance of pleasure over pain that that consideration

5. This is not, in my view, a very plausible version of desire theory. For arguments against it, see Mark Schroeder, *Slaves of the Passions*, pp. 97–102, 123–44. Although Schroeder defends a desire theory, he rejects this version, which he calls "proportionalism."

indicates that the action would yield. Other teleological accounts, which locate the normative force of reasons in the production of some good other than pleasure, would have this same structure.

These theories offer what might be called atomistic accounts of reasons and their strength. They explain the normative force of a reason with an amount of something—such as motivational force, or increments of pleasure and pain or some other good—that is associated with it.[6] None of these views seems to me plausible. As I have explained in previous lectures, I do not believe that agents always have reason to do what will satisfy their desires or preferences. There are indeed cases in which my reasons for choosing among certain options are determined by the degree to which I would enjoy them. And there are other cases in which the strength of reasons seems to be correlated with amounts of something. In some cases, for example, my reasons for choosing among certain courses of action may be, within limits, determined by amounts of money (by what different sellers charge for the same good, or by the amounts I would get paid for doing the same work). But these cases are special.

It is a mistake to generalize from these cases and to suppose that even if desire theories and hedonistic theories are to be rejected, there still must be some property the amount of which determines the strength of reasons for action. Given the heterogeneity of natural properties that can provide reasons it is not plausible to suppose that there is some natural property, amounts of which determine the relative strength of all reasons. It might be suggested that even if there is no such natural property, there is a normative property that plays this role. For example, it might be held that reasons for action are provided by the amount of value that an action would yield, and that the relative strengths of different reasons is explained by the differing amounts of value that they indicate an action would produce.

This view may sound plausible, but it should be rejected.[7] Not all reasons for action derive from the value of the states of affairs that those actions would yield. I have good reasons to put in time studying music, for example, even though the results of my amateurish efforts

---

6. Jonathan Dancy uses the term, "atomism," in a similar sense, as denoting the view that the normative force of a consideration that is a reason is a property that it carries with it in any context. See *Ethics Without Principles*, pp. 7 and 49–95. He also suggests that the appeal of atomism derives from desire theories of reasons. *Ethics Without Principles*, p. 75.

7. As I argue in Chapter 2 of *What We Owe to Each Other*.

could hardly be considered valuable. It might be said that these reasons are provided by the satisfaction and enjoyment I derive from this activity. But I would not enjoy it, or find the results satisfying, if I did not think music worth studying. If this belief were mistaken, then the reason provided by any pleasure I derive would be undermined. This illustrates a larger point that not all values are plausibly understood in terms of reasons to promote what is valuable. The fact that music, or physics, is valuable consists in part in the fact that these are things we have sufficient reason to study, even when doing so is tedious or difficult. Similarly, seeing my relationship with a friend as valuable involves, among other things, seeing myself as having conclusive reason to help him, even when this involves some sacrifice.[8]

These examples also indicate the case for understanding the relations SR and CR as holding of particular reasons, p, rather than just as holding when an agent "*has* sufficient (or conclusive) reason" for a certain action. We need to make claims about particular considerations being sufficient reason (and not being sufficient reason) for action in the presence of other, contrary reasons in order to express the content of various values.

I conclude that there is no non-normative or normative coin, in terms of which the strengths of reasons, considered on their own apart from comparison with other particular reasons, can be expressed, and which then serves as a basis for comparative judgments of the kind involved in relations such as SR and CR. The strength of a reason is an essentially comparative notion, understood only in relation to other particular reasons.

My account of strength is thus top-down rather than atomistic. It holds that insofar as there are facts about the relative strength of

---

8. These examples illustrate the difference between what Joshua Gert calls justifying strength and requiring strength. (See *Brute Rationality*, pp. 66–8.) My reason to study music has justifying strength (it makes this something I have sufficient reason to do) whereas my reason to help my friend has requiring strength (it makes helping him something I am rationally required to do). I agree with Gert in taking strength to be an essentially comparative notion, and I agree that there is a distinction between the cases he mentions. But I would not describe this as a distinction between different ways in which a consideration can count in favor of an action. What these cases illustrate is, rather, just two kinds of claims we can make about reasons using the normative relation, SR. My reason to study music is a sufficient reason to do so (at least in many circumstances). By contrast, the sense in which I am "rationally required" to help my friend just consists in the fact that in circumstances in which doing a would help my friend, most considerations, q are not sufficient reason to fail to help him.

reasons, these facts are fully captured by normative relations such as SR and CR, which express general principles about the roles properly given to certain considerations in deciding what to do and in justifying one's actions. It is a further question whether strength is, fundamentally, a matter of relations of outweighing, or whether we can make judgments of the relative strengths of non-competing reasons not based on their ability to outweigh other considerations. I believe that the former is the case, and that the counterfactual account I offered above of the strength of reasons for the same action is therefore not objectionably "indirect." It captures all of the potential significance that such comparisons have: as noting differences in the ways that these considerations might be outweighed by reasons for competing courses of action. The idea of the strength of a reason has no significance for us apart from consideration of such potential conflicts.

In an important respect, this top-down view resembles Kant's. Accepting that $SR(p, x, c, a)$ is what Kant called adopting a maxim, the policy of taking p to be sufficient reason for doing a in circumstances c. Kant seems to me to be correct in holding that maxims are fundamental elements of practical reasoning, although we differ about how these are to be interpreted. I understand maxims as judgments about the relative strength of reasons. For reasons that I mentioned in discussing expressivism in Lecture 3, I do not think that the content of a judgment that $SR(p, x, c, a)$ can be simply identified with a policy of giving priority to p in one's decisions about what to do in circumstances c. This fails to account for the significance that the fact that $SR(p, x, c, a)$ has in contexts other than individual decision-making, such as in justifications of one's actions to others and in giving advice.

Where I most clearly differ from Kant, however, is on the question of how we should decide which maxims to adopt, or, as I would put it, decide when it is the case that $SR(p, x, c, a)$ or that $CR(p, x, c, a)$. According to Kant, as I read him, a person (correctly) decides which maxims to adopt on the basis of his or her inclinations, under the constraints of the Categorical Imperative. I do not accept Kant's arguments for the Categorical Imperative as a fundamental principle of practical reasoning, and I do not want to say that the strength of reasons is in general determined by the strength of the agent's desires or by any other atomistic account. So I need to say something more about how we arrive at conclusions about the strength of reasons. I do not have a general answer to this question, but I will describe a few ways of arriving at conclusions about strength, that is to say, about which considerations outweigh others as reasons for action, that seem to me to be valid.

2. Consider first what I will call *quantitative* cases in which, on the surface, something like an atomistic view seems most plausible. If two dealers offer exactly the same model automobile, with the same warranty, but dealer A offers this at a lower price than dealer B, then the fact that A offers the car at this price gives one a stronger reason to buy it from him rather than from dealer B. But this conclusion depends on certain assumptions: that price is the only relevant difference between the two, and that the difference in price is significant. Once these assumptions are in place the normative conclusion follows, that I would be open to rational criticism for spending money needlessly by buying the car from dealer B.

These two normative assumptions are not comparative, let alone quantitative. The claim that the difference in money is significant is only the claim that it provides a reason for buying the car from dealer A unless there is some reason not to (i.e. the claim that this reason is not optional in the stronger sense mentioned above). It does not say anything about how this reason would compare with possible countervailing reasons. So the comparison of "amounts" occurs only at the non-normative level.

Looked at in this way, the example of buying the car is also an instance of a broader class of dominance cases, which are not necessarily quantitative. Suppose that my friend needs help and that either of two courses of action, C and D, would provide the needed help to the same degree. Doing C, however, would also help my business and my political career by getting my name in the newspaper. If there are no other reasons relevant to the choice between C and D, and if the advantage of getting my name in the newspapers provides a significant (i.e. non-optional) reason in this context, then it would seem that I have stronger reason to do C (i.e. that I would be open to rational criticism for ignoring this reason and doing D instead). Again, this seems to be a way of arriving at conclusions about relative strength without doing anything that looks like comparing the "weights" of the particular reasons involved. (I will later question one of the normative premises that this reasoning relies on.)

A third class of ways of arriving at conclusions about the relative strength of reasons involves what I will call *multilevel* cases. All of these involve general policies of giving some reasons priority over others in particular cases of certain kinds, which are justified by reasons for *having* these general policies rather than by comparisons of reasons provided by the factors at stake in particular cases. Sometimes the justification for these policies is instrumental. In order to lose weight by dieting, or to become healthier through exercise, one needs to have a general policy of giving greater weight to following one's diet or exercise plan than to (at least most of) the considerations of pleasure or convenience that provide reasons for deviating from this plan on a given day. This involves accepting general judgments of the form SR and CR. Although these judgments are not based on comparison of the reasons provided by the particular alternative one is choosing between on a given day, they do depend on background judgments of a comparative character: that the advantages of weight loss or greater fitness are worth the cost in pleasure and comfort. I am not trying to show that we never make comparative judgments about the strength of reasons—quite the contrary. My point is rather that we arrive at such judgments in a variety of different ways, which are not helpfully described as "weighing" the independent strengths of underlying considerations.[9]

The justification for comparative judgments in multilevel cases is not always instrumental. In the example I just gave of dominance reasoning the comparative judgment that one has conclusive reason to help one's friend, even at some personal cost, is a judgment required by being a friend. This is not to say that one accepts this judgment in order to bring it about that one is a good friend, as in the diet and exercise cases one follows a policy in order to bring it about that one loses weight, or is more physically fit. The idea is rather that being a good friend involves, among other things, taking certain views of the reasons one has. For example, one would not be a good friend if one did not give priority to one's friend's needs in this way. And it may also be the case that a good friend would not decide how to help his friend by considering what would be most advantageous to his own career, as in my previous example.[10]

9. Thus explaining how my view differs from what Selim Berker calls "the generalized weighing model." See Berker, "Particular Reasons."

10. These are good examples of arriving at conclusions about relation R (about which considerations are reasons at all) in a top-down (in this case a "multilevel") manner.

There is, of course, the further question of whether one has sufficient reason to be a friend at all. (This is why it is a multilevel case.)
Even if one is not a friend for the sake of the advantages this brings to
one's life, it must at least be true that the burdens of friendship do not
provide conclusive reasons against it, as they would in the case of a
relationship that involved allowing every aspect of one's life to be dic-
tated by the other person.

Moral reasons, which are often cited as examples of reasons with
special strength, are best understood on this multilevel, relationship
model. Particular moral principles, such as ones requiring fidelity to
promises, or forbidding acts that cause harm to others, are judgments
that certain considerations provide conclusive reasons for (or against)
certain actions in certain circumstances. Being moral involves holding
these judgments, just as being a friend involves seeing oneself as having
special reason to help one's friend when the need arises. There is then
the further question of what reason one has to hold these judgments
and try to live by them—i.e. what reason one has to take morality seriously. I believe that the best answer to this question lies in the fact that
they are required by a relationship with other rational beings that one
has reason to want, specifically, the relationship of seeing them as beings
to whom justification is owed. To fully defend the judgments of priority among reasons that moral principles involve, one must argue, as in
the case of friendship, that the burdens of accepting these judgments
are not so great as to make it unreasonable to hold them.[11]

3. The emphasis I have placed on general principles—moral principles
and other principles about reasons and the priority among them—
raises a question of how my view is related to particularism, understood as the denial that there are any such general practical principles.[12]
I have said that statements such as claims that $R(p, x, c, a)$, $SR(p, x, c, a)$,
or $CR(p, x, c, a)$, express general practical principles—general because
they claim that in any situations of type c, p is a reason, or a sufficient
reason, or a conclusive reason, to do a. It may seem to follow that the
position I am advocating is incompatible with particularism. On the

---

11. I offer a defense of this claim in *What We Owe to Each Other*, pp. 160–8.
12. Particularism is often stated as a view about *moral* principles, but I am assuming that
particularists such as Jonathan Dancy would say the same thing about practical principles more generally. What I have to say here would, I believe, carry over to the case
of moral principles.

other hand, by making explicit the fact that reasons and their strengths depend on circumstances, my view may seem to endorse one of the basic claims that particularists make.

Particularists assert that whether some consideration is a reason for or against a given action, and the strength that reason has, will depend on the agent's circumstances.[13] This seems obviously correct. The fact that there is a bomb under x's desk that will kill x unless he or she leaves the room now is in most circumstances sufficient, or even conclusive reason for x to leave the room now. But if x is a member of the resistance who knows that she is about to be captured by the occupying forces, will be tortured, and may not be able to resist revealing information about her confederates, then the fact just mentioned is sufficient reason for her *not* to leave the room.[14]

From the fact that the reason-giving status of a consideration varies with the circumstances it does not follow that there are no valid and meaningful practical principles. Particularists sometimes say that what they are denying is that there are valid, meaningful practical principles that are finitely specifiable, the idea being that given any finite specification of the conditions under which some consideration is held to be a reason, or a sufficient reason, for a certain action, we can always imagine a further factor which, if it were to obtain, would undercut that reason or alter its strength.

We might try to specify a general principle to cover the bomb examples I just mentioned by incorporating into the circumstances, c, the condition that the agent has good reason to want to go on living. But this is not enough. Even if x has good reason to want to go on living, he or she might have strong reasons for not leaving the room. For example, x might be a teacher who, by staying in the room longer, can help more of the children in his or her class to escape. So one would need to add the condition that x has no sufficient reason for remaining in the room.

Making these qualifications explicit weakens the principle. The last condition, that x does not have sufficient reason for remaining in the room, may seem to make what at first seemed to be a meaningful principle, holding that x has conclusive reason to leave the room, into a trivial claim that the presence of the bomb is conclusive reason for x to leave the room *if* he or she does not have sufficient reason to remain.

---

13. This is the thesis that Dancy calls holism. See *Ethics Without Principles*, p. 73.
14. An example suggested by the film about the French Resistance, *Army of Shadows*.

One way to strengthen the principle would be to restate these conditions in non-normative terms. Rather than saying that the agent has reason to want to go on living, we might specify that the agent is in good health and is not about to be killed in some other way, or subjected to great pain or suffering. Whether or not this is adequate, it would be much more difficult to spell out in non-normative terms the condition that the agent not have good reason to remain in the room. The range of possible obligations or other aims that might provide such reasons are too varied to be easily summarized.

This brings out a difference between claims involving the relation R and those involving SR and CR. Many valid claims that $R(p, x, c, a)$ can be formulated by specifying c in finite, non-normative terms. But, because claims about sufficient or conclusive reasons must take conflicting reasons into account, and because the range of possible conflicting reasons is so wide, claims about the relations SR and CR are unlikely to be finitely expressible in non-normative terms. What is special about judgments about particular cases is that in a particular case we can know what factors could provide possible conflicting reasons, and we can therefore determine whether the normative conditions that would be included in the specification of c in a general principle are fulfilled or not.

If general practical principles include conditions specified in normative terms, so that "applying" them involves making judgments about what reasons we have, why should we be concerned with these principles? The most important answer is that we cannot avoid doing so as long as we think at all about what reasons we have, since every conclusion about our reasons for action is a general principle of this kind. Beyond this, as I said in Lecture 4, the process of reflection on these principles is a process of coming to a better understanding of the reasons we take ourselves to have. We may, for example, take the prospect of a certain kind of pleasure to be a reason for acting in a certain way in a particular case. But reflection is required to spell out what features of the case are essential to making this true. Our future practical thinking will reflect the conclusions we reach through this process, not in general because we are constrained to follow these principles, but simply because we continue to see the conclusions they express as being correct.

Particularism is most often stated as a view about *moral* principles. Like the practical principles I have been discussing, moral principles are often finitely stable only in terms that are in part normative. For example, if a person has promised to do something, then he or she is obligated to fulfill this promise unless it was made involuntarily. But the relevant notion of voluntariness is itself normative. It cannot be identified with a psychological condition of being in accord with the promisor's will, or with the idea of having "acceptable alternatives." The latter interpretation would not distinguish between a promise to pay the robber who says, "Your money or your life," and a promise to pay a surgeon for a life-saving operation, since in each case the alternative to the promise may be a prompt and painful death.[15] To distinguish these cases we need a larger moral framework specifying what people are obligated to provide for one another and what they are entitled to withhold. (If the promise to the surgeon is morally questionable it is not simply because the agent's life is at stake but because, like the robber, the surgeon is demanding something he or she is not entitled to demand.)

These moral conditions do not make the moral principle of fidelity to promises trivial or useless. Such conditions might seem to be a problem because moral principles are a response to our need to have general expectations about how people are going to behave toward one another in certain important respects. They claim to be standards we have reason to follow, and are supposed to serve as the basis for interpersonal criticism and justification. It may seem that they cannot play this role if further moral reasoning is required in order to see what they require in individual cases.

But this is not the case, for at least two reasons. First, principles incorporating normative, or even moral, conditions can serve as a shared standard of conduct and justification because we share a clear enough idea of what the non-normative conditions are that fulfill those conditions in most cases. We should just not take a particular specification of these non-normative conditions as capturing the full content of the relevant principles. So, for example, we share a sense of what conditions generally render a promise voluntary or involuntarily in the relevant sense. But when difficult cases arise we need to be guided by a deeper understanding of the relevant moral framework: an

---

15. As Hume pointed out in *A Treatise of Human Nature*, Book III, Part II, Section V. I discuss the question of how voluntariness should be understood in Chapter 6 of *What We Owe to Each Other*, and in "Responsibility and the Value of Choice."

understanding of why promises generally obligate and why there has to be an exception for promises made involuntarily.

Second, when we reflect on a principle, and ask ourselves what that principle requires, we are *always* engaging in moral reasoning, not just deriving a conclusion from some given rule. This is true in clear cases as well as in difficult ones. To see a principle as having "moral force" in a given case always involves seeing what it requires as the content of a justifiable set of interpersonal standards.

Turning now from the case of moral principles to the general case of principles about reasons for action, I have said that judgments about normative relations such as R, SR, and CR involve general principles about the reasons we have. These principles may seem to differ from moral principles in two related ways. First, the point of such principles is not to serve as interpersonal standards of justification and criticism. Second, unlike moral principles, these principles are not standards that we have some further reason to follow, but simply conclusions about our reasons for acting one way or another. We "follow" such principles by deliberating and acting in ways that are in accord with them, but they do not constrain us, as moral principles may be thought to do.

There is something right about each of these contrasts, but the differences should not be exaggerated. First, general principles about reasons for action are not formulated to serve as standards of interpersonal justification. But, in addition to serving as the basis of explanation and advice, these principles play a crucial role in our moral thinking, in my view. As I indicated in Lecture 4, in discussing moral constructivism, conclusions about moral right and wrong depend on conclusions about what individuals in certain circumstances have reason to want and to do.

Second, it makes sense to ask what reason we have to do what morality requires in a way that it does not *in general* make sense to ask what reason we have to do what we have concluded that we have reason to do. So one might, as I have said, conclude that moral principles are standards that constrain us in a way that conclusions about reasons for action—expressing general practical principles—do not. But this contrast does not always hold, and the idea of constraint can be misleading.

Constraint in the relevant sense can occur whenever what one has conclusive reason to do runs counter to some psychologically significant source of motivation. This is a perfectly general phenomenon, not limited to cases of moral obligation. Moreover, when the judgment that one has this conclusive reason is arrived at through multilevel reasoning, it makes sense to ask for a reason for giving priority to this consideration. One is not asking (incoherently) for a reason for doing what one has reason to do, but rather asking (coherently) why a particular consideration *is* a conclusive reason. This experience of constraint is familiar from cases such as the examples of diet and exercise in which the relevant explanation is instrumental. "Constraint" by moral principles is, like loyalty to one's friends, just a non-instrumental version of the same thing. So the constraint involved is a general rational phenomenon rather than distinctively moral.

4. In my first lecture I listed seven questions about reasons that seemed to require answers. In addition to questions about optionality and strength, which I have just discussed, these were:

Relational Character: Reasons are reasons *for* an agent. How is this relational character to be understood?

Determinate Truth Values: Are statements about reasons true or false, independent of our opinions about them? Does the idea that there are irreducibly normative truths of this kind have unacceptable metaphysical implications?

Supervenience: How are facts about reasons related to natural facts? They are not entailed by natural facts, but cannot vary unless natural facts vary. This seems puzzling, and in need of explanation.

Knowledge: If there are irreducibly normative facts about reasons, how can we come to know such facts?

Practical Significance: Judgments about reasons play a different role than other beliefs—such as beliefs about the natural world—in practical reasoning and in the explanation of action. How can they play this role if they are beliefs?

I will conclude this final lecture by reviewing the answers I have offered to these questions. I have taken what may seem to be a short way with the first question, by asserting that the basic elements in normative judgments are relations, such as the relation $R(p, x, c, a)$, which holds when a consideration p is a reason for an agent in circumstances c to do action a. This thesis seems to me to have considerable explanatory value. The relational character of reasons is most likely to seem puzzling if we focus on reasons *themselves*, that is to say the states of affairs, p, that stand in this relation to agents and their actions. If we take the basic normative claims to be apparently non-relational claims that these things "are reasons," or similar apparently non-relational claims that certain things "are good," then the question naturally arises what these normative facts have to do with *us*. (This puzzlement lies behind Christine Korsgaard's caricature when she says that according to a realist view reasons are normative entities that we notice "as it were, wafting by."[16]) The idea that the basic elements of the normative domain are relations avoids this puzzlement. Truths about reasons are truths about relations that hold between *us* (as individuals in certain circumstances) and certain other facts (often but not always non-normative facts). So the question "What do normative facts have to do with us?" has an obvious answer. The idea that normative facts are relational in this way does not seem to me ad hoc, but quite natural once one thinks of it. It also explains other features of normative truths.

In particular, as I have argued, it provides the basis for a plausible interpretation of the "fact/value distinction," and explains the puzzling aspect of the phenomenon of supervenience, namely the fact that many normative truths co-vary with non-normative truths even though they are not entailed by them. More exactly, it explains why those normative facts *that vary at all*, co-vary with non-normative facts even though they are not entailed by them. This relation holds in virtue of the truth of what I called pure normative truths, which assign normative significance to non-normative facts. These pure normative truths themselves, however, do not vary.

I also took what may have seemed to be a short way with the question of motivation, or, as I would call it, the question of normative significance. I said that it is part of being a rational agent that one's beliefs about what one has reason to do generally influence one's subsequent behavior, and can explain that behavior. Building this connection between belief and action into the concept of a rational agent may seem question-begging. But it should not seem so. All of the non-cognitivist views that are alternatives to mine explain the relation between normative judgment and action by appealing to some psychological ideal type: an agent who (normally) responds to the imperatives he or she issues, an agent who (normally) carries out the plans he or she has made, and so on. The difference lies only in the particular psychological ideal type appealed to. There seems to me no reason to prefer these alternatives to the one I propose, given that, as

16. *The Sources of Normativity*, p. 44.

I argued in Lectures 2 and 4, there are no metaphysical or epistemological objections to taking normative judgments to be capable of
truth and possible objects of belief and knowledge. The fact that a
cognitivist account provides a more natural and attractive interpretation of our view of our own reasons and of interpersonal argument
about reasons is, moreover, a ground for preferring it.

I argued in Lecture 2 that the idea that there are irreducibly normative truths about practical reasons does not have metaphysical implications that we should find troubling. I defended this claim within a
general domain-centered account of ontological questions. Claims
within a given domain give rise to external ontological questions only
if the truth or significance of those claims requires that the facts or
entities they refer to are part of a "world" that is understood independently of that domain. These questions are troubling if our understanding of that world gives reason to believe that no such things could be
part of it. But normative truths have no such external implications or
presuppositions. The truth of such claims and their significance for us
are entirely accounted for in terms internal to that domain—that is, in
normative terms. The same is true of mathematical truths, such as
truths of set theory.

In both cases there remain the questions of whether statements
within these domains have determinate truth values independent of us,
and of how we can come to know what these truth values are. The best
response to the question of determinateness, I argued, would be a suit-
ably general account of the domain in question in the terms of that
domain itself (in normative, or in mathematical terms). This would
respond to the epistemological question as well, by characterizing the
kind of thinking through which we can discover truths about that
domain. Since such an account would itself be a general normative or
mathematical claim, there is the question of how we could come to
know it. The method of reflective equilibrium is an adequate answer
to this question unless the best understanding of the domain holds that
facts about it are somehow inaccessible to us. I have argued that this is
not true of either normative or mathematical facts.

It seems to me that there is some prospect of attaining an overall
account of set theory of the kind I have described. But I see no prospect of doing this for normative judgments in general or judgments
about reasons for action in particular. The only way we have of establishing the truth of normative judgments is through direct, piecemeal

application of the method of reflective equilibrium. This method can provide us with justified confidence in the truth of some judgments about reasons for action, and hence with justified confidence that questions of this kind can have determinate answers. But it provides no assurance that such questions always have such answers. Whether this is so in any given case will depend on the outcome of this method when applied to that case.

Christine Korsgaard has written that on a substantive realist account of reasons we have nothing more to go on than our confidence that, after thinking about what reasons we have, we have gotten it right.[17] She intends this as a criticism of a view of the kind I have been defending. But her description of our situation seems to me generally correct. We do have nothing to rely on except our best *judgments* about which things are reasons, although our confidence in these judgments can be justified in the ways I have described. There is nothing more that we could ask for. To be realistic about reasons we must accept this fact.

17. *The Sources of Normativity*, p. 40.

Bibliography

Benacerraf, Paul, "Mathematical Truth," in Benacerraf and Putnam, pp. 403–20.

—— and Hilary Putnam, eds, *The Philosophy of Mathematics*, second edition (Cambridge: Cambridge University Press, 1983).

Berker, Selim, "Particular Reasons," *Ethics* 118 (2007), pp. 109–39.

Blackburn, Simon, "Errors and the Phenomenology of Value," in *Essays in Quasi-Realism*, pp. 149–65.

—— *Essays in Quasi-Realism* (Oxford: Oxford University Press, 1993).

—— "How to be an Ethical Anti-Realist," in *Essays in Quasi-Realism*, pp. 166–81.

—— "Moral Realism," in *Essays in Quasi-Realism,* pp. 111–30.

—— *Ruling Passions* (Oxford: Oxford University Press, 1998).

—— "Supervenience Revisited," in *Essays in Quasi-Realism*, pp. 130–48.

Boolos, George, "Iteration Again," *Philosophical Topics* 42 (1989), pp. 5–21.

—— "The Iterative Conception of Set," in Benacerraf and Putnam, pp. 487–502.

Brandt, Richard, *A Theory of the Good and the Right* (Oxford: Clarendon Press, 1979).

Broome, John, "Does Rationality Consist in Responding Correctly to Reasons?," *Journal of Moral Philosophy* 4 (2007), pp. 349–74.

Burge, Tyler, *Origins of Objectivity* (Oxford: Clarendon Press, 2010).

Carnap, Rudolph, "Empiricism, Semantics, and Ontology," in *Meaning and Necessity: A Study in Semantics and Modal Logic* (Chicago: University of Chicago Press, 1956), pp. 205–21.

Cuneo, Terence, *The Normative Web* (Oxford: Oxford University Press, 2007).

Dancy, Jonathan, *Ethics Without Principles* (Oxford: Oxford University Press, 2004).

Davidson, Donald, "Actions, Reasons, and Causes," in *Essays on Actions and Events* (Oxford: Clarendon Press, 1980), pp. 3–19.

Dreier, Jamie, "Meta-ethics and the Problem of Creeping Minimalism," *Philosophical Perspectives* 18 (2004), pp. 23–44.

Dworkin, Ronald, *Justice for Hedgehogs* (Cambridge, MA: Harvard University Press, 2011).

Egan, Andy, "Quasi-Realism and Fundamental Moral Error," *Australasian Journal of Philosophy* 85 (2007), pp, 205–19.

Enoch, David, *Taking Morality Seriously* (Oxford: Oxford University Press, 2011).

Feferman, Solomon, "Conceptions of the Continuum," *Intellectica* 51 (2009), pp. 169–89.

Field, Hartry, "Platonism for Cheap? Crispin Wright on Frege's Context Principle," in his *Realism, Mathematics and Modality* (Oxford: Basil Blackwell, 1991), pp. 147–70.

Fine, Kit, "The Varieties of Necessity," in Tamar Szabó Gendler and John Hawthorne, eds, *Conceivability and Possibility* (New York: Oxford University Press, 2002), pp. 253–81.

Foot, Philippa, *Natural Goodness* (Oxford: Oxford University Press, 2001).

Freeman, Samuel, ed., *The Cambridge Companion to Rawls* (Cambridge: Cambridge University Press, 2003).

Gert, Joshua, *Brute Rationality: Normativity and Human Action* (Cambridge: Cambridge University Press, 2007).

——"Normative Strength and the Balance of Reasons," *The Philosophical Review* 116 (2007), pp. 533–62.

Gibbard, Allan, *Thinking How to Live* (Cambridge, MA: Harvard University Press, 2003).

——*Wise Choices, Apt Feelings* (Cambridge, MA: Harvard University Press, 1990).

Gödel, Kurt, "What Is Cantor's Continuum Problem?," in Benacerraf and Putnam, pp. 470–85.

Goodman, Nelson, *Fact, Fiction, and Forecast* (Cambridge, MA: Harvard University Press, 1953).

Hare, R. M., *The Language of Morals* (Oxford: Oxford University Press, 1952).

Harman, Gilbert, "Moral Relativism Defended," *Philosophical Review* 84 (1975), pp. 3–22.

——*The Nature of Morality* (New York: Oxford University Press, 1977).

——"Notes on Practical Reasoning," <http://www.princeton.edu/~harman/Papers/SPAWN.pdf> (2007).

Hume, David, *A Treatise of Human Nature*, ed. L. A. Selby-Bigge (Oxford: Oxford University Press, 1968 (1739)).

Jackson, Frank, *From Metaphysics to Ethics* (Oxford: Oxford University Press, 1998).

Kelly, Thomas, "Peer Disagreement and Higher Order Evidence," in Richard Feldman and Ted A. Warfield, eds, *Disagreement* (Oxford: Oxford University Press, 2010), pp. 111–74.

——and Sarah McGrath, "Is Reflective Equilibrium Enough?," *Philosophical Perspectives* 24 (2010), pp. 325–59.

Koellner, Peter, "Truth in Mathematics: The Question of Pluralism," in Otávio Bueno and Øystein Linnebo, eds, *New Waves in Philosophy of Mathematics* (New York: Palgrave Macmillan, 2009), pp. 80–116.

Kolodny, Niko, "Aims as Reasons," in Samuel Freeman, Rahul Kumar, and R. Jay Wallace, eds, *Reasons and Recognition: Essays on the Philosophy of T. M. Scanlon* (New York: Oxford University Press, 2011), pp. 43–78.

Korsgaard, Christine, "Acting for a Reason," in *The Constitution of Agency*, pp. 201–29.

—— *The Constitution of Agency* (Oxford: Oxford University Press, 2008).

——"The Normativity of Instrumental Reason," in *The Constitution of Agency*, pp. 27–68.

—— *Self-Constitution: Agency, Identity, and Integrity* (Oxford: Oxford University Press, 2009).

—— *The Sources of Normativity* (Cambridge: Cambridge University Press, 1996).

Mackie, John, *Ethics: Inventing Right and Wrong* (Harmondsworth: Penguin Books, 1977).

McDowell, John, "Non-Cognitivism and Rule Following," in Steven Holzman and Christopher Leich, eds, *Wittgenstein: To Follow a Rule* (London: Routledge, 1981), pp. 141–62.

——"Values and Secondary Qualities," in Ted Honderich, ed., *Morality and Objectivity* (London: Routledge & Kegan Paul, 1985), pp. 110–29.

Nagel, Thomas, *The Possibility of Altruism* (Oxford: Oxford University Press, 1970).

—— *The View from Nowhere* (Oxford: Oxford University Press, 1987).

Nietzsche, Friedrich, *On the Genealogy of Morality*, ed. Maudemarie Clark and Alan J. Swensen (Indianapolis: Hackett Publishing, 1998).

O'Neill, Onora, *Constructions of Reason* (Cambridge: Cambridge University Press, 1989).

Parfit, Derek, "Justifiability to Each Other," in Philip Stratton-Lake, ed., *On What We Owe to Each Other* (Oxford: Blackwell Publishing, 2004), pp. 67–89.

—— *On What Matters* (Oxford: Oxford University Press, 2011).

Parsons, Charles, *Mathematical Thought and Its Objects* (Cambridge: Cambridge University Press, 2008).

——"What Is the Iterative Conception of Set?," in Benaceraf and Putnam, pp. 503–29.

Prior, A. N., "The Autonomy of Ethics," *Australasian Journal of Philosophy* 38 (1960), pp. 199–206.

Putnam, Hilary, *The Collapse of the Fact/Value Dichotomy* (Cambridge, MA: Harvard University Press, 2002).

—— *Ethics without Ontology* (Cambridge, MA: Harvard University Press, 2004).

Quine, Willard, *The Pursuit of Truth* (Cambridge, MA: Harvard University Press, 1990).

Quinn, Warren, "Putting Rationality in its Place," in his *Morality and Action* (Cambridge: Cambridge University Press, 1993), pp. 228–55.

Rawls, John, *A Theory of Justice* (Cambridge, MA: Harvard University Press, 1971).

——*Collected Papers*, ed. Samuel Freeman (Cambridge, MA: Harvard University Press, 1999).

——"The Independence of Moral Theory," in *Collected Papers*, pp. 286–302.

——"Kantian Constructivism in Moral Theory," in *Collected Papers*, pp. 303–58.

——"An Outline of a Decision Procedure for Ethics," in *Collected Papers*, pp. 1–19.

——*Political Liberalism* (New York: Columbia University Press, 1993).

Raz, Joseph, *Engaging Reason* (Oxford: Oxford University Press, 1999).

——"Incommensurability and Agency," in *Engaging Reason*, pp. 46–67.

——*The Morality of Freedom* (Oxford: Oxford University Press, 1986).

——"The Myth of Instrumental Rationality," *Journal of Ethics and Social Philosophy* 1 (2005), pp. 1–28.

——"Reasons: Practical and Adaptive," in David Sobel and Steven Wall, eds, *Reasons for Action* (Cambridge: Cambridge University Press, 2009), pp. 37–57.

Rippon, Simon, *An Epistemological Argument for Moral Response-Dependence* (PhD dissertation, Harvard University 2010).

Rosen, Gideon, "Blackburn's *Essays in Quasi-Realism*," *Nous* 32 (1998), pp. 386–405.

Scanlon, T. M., "How I am not a Kantian," in Parfit, *On What Matters*, Volume Two, pp. 116–39.

——"Rawls on Justification," in Freeman, ed., *The Cambridge Companion to Rawls*, pp. 139–67.

——"Reasons: A Puzzling Duality?," in R. Jay Wallace, Philip Pettit, Samuel Scheffler, and Michael Smith, eds, *Reason and Value: Themes from the Moral Philosophy of Joseph Raz* (Oxford: Oxford University Press, 2004), pp. 231–46.

——"Responsibility and the Value of Choice," *Think* 12 (2013), pp. 9–16.

——"Structural Irrationality," in Geoffrey Brennan, Robert Goodin, Frank Jackson, and Michael Smith, eds, *Common Minds: Essays in Honor of Philip Pettit* (Oxford: Oxford University Press, 2007), pp. 84–103.

——"The Unity of the Normative," *Philosophical Studies* 154 (2011), pp. 443–50.

——*What We Owe to Each Other* (Cambridge, MA: Harvard University Press, 1998).

——"Wrongness and Reasons: A Reexamination," in Russ Shafer-Landau, ed., *Oxford Studies in Metaethics, Vol 2* (Oxford: Oxford University Press, 2007), pp. 5–20.

Schroeder, Mark, *Slaves of the Passions* (Oxford: Oxford University Press, 2007).

Searle, John, *The Construction of Social Reality* (New York: The Free Press, 1995).

Shoenfield, J. R. "Axioms of Set Theory," in Jon Barwise, ed., *Handbook of Mathematical Logic* (Amsterdam: North Holland, 1977), pp. 321–44.

Skorupski, John, *The Domain of Reasons* (Oxford: Oxford University Press: 2010).

Smith, Michael, *The Moral Problem* (Oxford: Blackwell Publishers, 1994).

—— "Objectivity and Moral Realism: On the Significance of the Phenomenology of Moral Experience," in his *Ethics and the A Priori: Selected Essays on Moral Psychology and Meta-Ethics* (Cambridge: Cambridge University Press, 2004), pp. 234–58.

Street, Sharon, "A Darwinian Dilemma for Realist Theories of Value," in *Philosophical Studies* 127 (2006), pp. 109–66.

—— "In Defense of Future Tuesday Indifference: Ideally Coherent Eccentrics and the Contingency of What Matters," *Philosophical Issues* 19 (2009), pp. 273–98.

Tait, William W., "Beyond the Axioms: The Question of Objectivity in Mathematics," in his *The Provenance of Pure Reason*, pp. 89–104.

—— *The Provenance of Pure Reason: Essays in the Philosophy of Mathematics and Its History* (Oxford: Oxford University Press, 2005).

—— "Truth and Proof: The Platonism of Mathematics," in his *The Provenance of Pure Reason*, pp. 61–88.

Thomson, Judith, *Normativity* (Peru, IL: Open Court Publishing, 2008).

Wallace, R. Jay, "Normativity and the Will," in his *Normativity & the Will: Selected Essays on Moral Psychology and Practical Reason* (Oxford: Oxford University Press, 2006), pp. 71–81.

Williams, Bernard, *Ethics and the Limits of Philosophy* (Cambridge, MA: Harvard University Press, 1985).

—— "Internal and External Reasons," in his *Moral Luck* (Cambridge: Cambridge University Press, 1981), pp. 101–13.

—— "Replies," in J. E. J. Altham and Ross Harrison, eds, *World, Mind, and Ethics: Essays on the Ethical Philosophy of Bernard Williams* (Cambridge: Cambridge University Press, 1995), pp. 185–224.

Williamson, Timothy, *The Philosophy of Philosophy* (Malden, MA: Blackwell Publishing, 2007).

Wright, Crispin, *Frege's Conception of Numbers as Objects* (Aberdeen: Aberdeen University Press, 1983).

—— *Truth and Objectivity* (Cambridge, MA: Harvard University Press, 1992).

Index

Printed and bound by CPI Group (UK) Ltd, Croydon, CR0 4YY